Sixteen Chickens on a Trampoline

Faye Lippitt

CLM Publishing (Cayman Islands)

ISBN 978-1-629-038667
Copyright ©2014 by Faye Lippitt

Contact the author: Faye Lippitt:
gmalippitt@gmail.com

Published by CLM Publishing
www.shop.clmpublishing.com
Grand Cayman, Cayman Islands

Printed in the United States of America.

DEDICATION

For our gang of six. And Greg, who made you all possible.

The most important part of this book can be found at the end.

Those blank pages are for you, dear reader, to fill with those little gems that your child or grandchild says and does.

It is the stuff that love is made of.

Write it and remember.

Share your stories with Faye at 16chickens.com

CONTENTS

PREFACE

When my husband and I were raising our six children, people kept asking, "How do you do it?" Well, the same way folks all over the world have been doing it I guess, some with more, some with fewer kids. My mom was the eldest of fifteen born on a farm near Grandview, Manitoba, to Ukrainian immigrants. My grandmother managed the first five with no running water or electricity.

How did SHE do it?

I guess the simple answer is, "You just do what you can." Perhaps a more pertinent question would be to ask how you get through each day and still keep smiling.

Surely there is a skill, a trick, or an art we could master to help us through the day. For me, the skill was one that kids provide themselves; one we somehow forget we have when we get to be an adult and are faced with the stress of all the crying, storming, laughing little faces that surround us tightly and won't let go. It's quite simple really. Just pick out the funny parts. Kids always see the funny parts. And there are usually funny parts in most situations that deal with kids.

I began this book when I began having children. It started when I'd write down the funny things they would say, then progressed to the funny things they would do. And eventually these things became a lifeline for me when I was overcome by those tiny faces that surrounded me so tightly.

I'd try to withdraw from sticky situations; try to just sit back and think that surely if I wasn't so tired, so grumpy, so overwhelmed with the moment, I'd find this quite funny. So I'd write about it. I chose writing as a means to temporary sanity and would write about each insane situation because they were, I discovered, funny. I had in fact discovered the magic of choice: you can laugh or you can cry, and laughter feels so much better than tears.

I really began the book though, two days after our grand daughter was born, when I found myself emailing our son and telling him and his lovely wife to just remember to laugh when things get rough; that they could more easily clear the air with laughter. What they needed to do was just, kind of… rise above the situation and see it from a different perspective. When I did that, I liked to think I was watching with the angels. Maybe, as the Scottish saying goes, angels can fly because they take themselves lightly.

This book transcribes a voyage of about twenty years, from when our eldest, Alex, was a toddler to when our youngest, Elly, was fourteen. It details those crazy years in between, when two sets of twins arrived and chaos reigned. The laughter didn't stop when the kids got older, but the chaos seemed to abate. Now, isn't it funny that from chaos sprang creativity?

Mind you if chaos is just a lot of unfocused energy flying around, it's no wonder that when that crazy energy ricochets into a person, the creative spirit is moved.

Good luck on the most precipitous and challenging voyage you'll ever under-take in your life: raising children.

This book is divided into stories I wrote about those many crazy events that I became very fond of, as well as shorter quotes from my diary that are dated when I remembered to do so. Of course there were many more, but sometimes I forgot to write them down and they have disappeared into a memory that fades with time.

"I have a great belief in the fact that whenever there is chaos, it creates wonderful thinking. I consider chaos a gift."

-Septima Poinsette Clark

INTRODUCTION

When I was in my twenties I didn't want kids. I wanted adventure, and found plenty of it in my travels. When - by the grace of God - I lived to reach thirty, I found myself married to a man who was interested in adventure too. So we started our family, which has proven to be the greatest adventure of our lives.

We had kids for a variety of reasons. Some that come to mind are: they are charming, they are very good educational tools and, if you are a creative person, they are the ultimate in creation, and a lasting one at that.

Surely the ultimate in creativity is drawing two lives together to make a new one. And you never know what you're going to get! Blonde, brunette or redhead? Mom's funny teeth? Dad's big feet? Athlete? Philosopher?

When it comes to the charming part, consider this: charm is not a random event occurring in some kids. It is a true Darwinian survival attribute. If the kids weren't so darn cute, you'd be tempted to toss them out at 2 a.m. with their pile of smelly diapers and booger-encrusted fist. However, just the sight of a pout or a toothless smile can melt a weary heart.

Nothing I learned at school or in my travels could compare with the education I received raising children. Children are mirrors of the soul. They reflect equally the good, the bad, the strong, the weak, the noble and the downright dark parts of each of us.

You see, whether you want it or not in this life, you always seem to get what you need. You're a bit uptight about cleanliness? You'll either get someone who wears one pair of shorts all summer long (day and night) or "She-Ra the Shower Nut", who jumps in the shower for thirty minutes when she gets ketchup on her fingers. And that's the easy grade-school stuff. Wait until you graduate to the tough ones: arrogance, stubbornness, impatience, greed, and self-deprecation. For any one of these features that you might harbor, there is a child that will embody it so obviously that you will not be able to ignore it. And it won't go away until you face it - in your child and in yourself.

No, it is definitely not an easy lesson, this other education, but it is by far the most worthwhile of all. For it is with children that one comes to understand the important things in life. What they need and what we need are the same: love, companionship, nurturing and acceptance.

When I'm in the last half of my life and I glance across a long table loaded with food in a room filled with laughter, I'll know the journey that Greg and I undertook was the right one for us - for love, once created, never ends.

Chapter 1

DISCIPLINE

To live a passionate life, a person has to feel passionately; has to loosen restraints of the heart that might have been placed there to protect from past assaults. Kids are great at this. Passionate they are! Try taking something away from them that they are particularly fascinated with and listen to the howl.

There are, however, societal restraints put there for the safety of the group that we (hopefully) observe. If we're to have a just and caring society, we have to model that to our kids. Aye, and there's the rub. The modeling part. The actual tricky part starts when we attempt to combine passion with the aforementioned modeling.

If we want the kids to behave in an acceptable fashion, there has to be a certain amount of discipline - there's just no escaping it. Fail to do it in the home, as in society, and chaos ensues. And when chaos reigns, as often happens when there are a lot of children bounding around, it is not always easy to keep your head and rein in your passion.

We're adults! When our kids are yelling, we're not supposed to yell back. Sure is tempting though. When they're clouting each other, we're not supposed to clout them back, for then we're just perpetuating what we're trying to avoid. Sure can be tempting though. I should know. I've yelled and clouted. I suppose you do teach what you need to learn.

Kenny Rogers sang a Don Schlitz song called *The Gambler*. I sometimes think it refers as much to raising kids as it does to card games. Having kids is always a gamble when you come to think of it. You never know what's going to happen next. Considering Kenny had almost as many wives (five) as he had children (six), maybe he had them all in mind when he sang his song.

Every parent will find a way to deal with discipline. I can only say what worked for us. It's kind of like Kenny said:

"If you're gonna play the game,
boy you gotta learn to play it right
You've got to know when to hold 'em
Know when to fold 'em
Know when to walk away
Know when to run."

"Hold them" and love them; "fold them" in your arms and smile; "walk" them to the corner or to their room for a time-out; or "run" for the great outdoors and breathe deeply when you are tempted to do something you'll regret.

We knew we needed to do something to keep our kids in line, but we also knew that just as each child was unique, so would each situation be different. We really didn't know what might work for all of them, yet fair's fair – they needed to know the outcome when they pushed too far. It's a gamble!

Eventually, we decided that the best way to discipline a child was the easiest. Get them to do the walking, so we could cool ourselves down and then figure out what to do next. Often banishing your youngin' from the herd is the simplest and easiest solution of all.

Thus, when our three year-old son Alex misbehaved, he was sent to his room. He marched off, paused and did a quick U-turn, then fired back, "You…pooperdag!"

I looked at Greg and muttered, "Did he just call me a pooperdag?"

"Yes. I believe he did."

"Wow, great word," I marveled. Very quietly.

"Don't judge each day by the harvest you reap but by the seeds that you plant."

-Robert Louis Stevenson

Chapter 2

IT'S TWINS! IT'S TWINS!

The first time I learned I was carrying twins, I raced out of the medical lab where I'd had the ultrasound and headed down the block, straight for my fitness class, exploded through the door, threw up my arms and yelled, "It's twins! It's twins!" to a stunned classroom of gyrating females. I then ran back to my old Datsun and beat it for home as fast as I could to tell my husband. Half way there I looked up, yelled, "Thanks God!" and started to cry.

When I got home I raced into my startled husband's arms and blubbered, "There's two! There's two!"

I think we danced around a bit, then phoned our moms. Guess you might say we were excited.

After we'd had a boy and girl to join our three-year-old firstborn son, many people said, "There. Now you're finished."

For a while we thought we were. Heaven knows those first months were not easy, but after a year or two, things seemed —well— not hectic enough. We were both from families of four children after all, so we thought we'd even things up and try again.

What our doctor didn't tell us was that if the mom happens to be over the age of thirty-five when this occurs, that the odds of having more than one at a time are considerably different. We learned — once we were pregnant— that those odds could be as high as fifty-fifty.

Perhaps it was not so odd then, that we did not even things at all. When we were told for the second time "There's two, there's two", excitement was replaced with amusement.

What the heck. At least there weren't three in there.

So. You usually have a choice. You can laugh or you can cry, and since crying is really no fun at all we chose laughter. We've laughed a lot since.

And cried.

Having two sets of twins — five children in six years— can do that to you. One moment tears of frustration and the next, unexpected giggles.

Once we had become accustomed to the fact that we'd be getting a double dose of "double your pleasure, double your fun", we began to tackle the extras that came with it.

First, we bought a new vehicle that was double the size of our car, which multiplied car payments by two.

We already had a lot of the necessary tools: a double stroller, two small beds, car seats. Some small premonition had kept me from getting rid of at least half of it long before.

Naming the new babies was another consideration. The older three decided it had to be Bert and Ernie. Our parents offered Pete and Repeat. Friends suggested that if it turned out to be triplets, to call them Eenie, Meenie and Miny ('cause you don't want no Mo).

We noticed an interesting change in neighbours and acquaintances at this time. Those who had once said,

"There, now you're finished," now asked hesitantly, "Um, are you going to continue?"

After five, we had seemingly entered the realm of the unusual and improbable. Anyone who could have five could just as believably go for ten, I suppose.

When our two wee boys arrived, followed a couple of years later by their sister, the realm of the unusual and improbable descended upon us. Ordinary outings became a study in logistics.

Take grocery shopping. You need two carts: one with babies stuffed in and hanging from, and the other with food in it. The hazards are not problems in steering, but rather problems with braking fast to avoid shoppers who stop dead in front of you and just stare.

I suppose one does that when seeing double.

1988:

February

Today is pancake Tuesday and so we are eating pancakes for dinner, much to the children's delight. When told that tomorrow is Lent and they are supposed to give something up, Jane quickly announced she would give up light bulbs. Charles's choice was mineral water. Alex was more cautious. After some deliberation he decided to give up spinach. Greg offered to give up work. I think I'll just give up.

May

Jane, dreamily from the couch: "Mom, what colour are ladybug footprints?"

Summer

Jane waltzed into the kitchen with her pal Claire who was suffering from a cold. I caught the tail end of their conversation...

"No no no. That just makes your arm sticky. You do it like this", and pointing her nose in the air she continued, "You gotta sniff them boo-boos" —giving a very credible sniff— "like that."

September

As I helped Charles and Jane change their clothes one day, I absently said, "Here you two, I'm going to help you out". Charles shot back, "No! We don't want out. Why do we haf ta go out again?"

Chapter 3

THE MALL

City kids hang out in malls. At least that is what country kids think.

Our nearest mall consists of a country store that features everything a mall does, only instead of stores offering different merchandise, there are shelves offering a variety of stuff. Beside the crackers and under the soap you'll find cat food, which is next to the Band-Aids.

Our eldest was only six when he decided that it was time to expand his horizons. He'd seen the advertisements on TV. It was time, he insisted, that we visited Kid Mecca. It was time for a trip to West Edmonton Mall.

We had just welcomed our second set of twins into the world three months earlier to join their three-year-old brother and sister, and afore-mentioned six-year-old brother. Thinking that perhaps our eldest had been neglected in the dizzy, demanding days of late, we gave in and decided to spend a weekend in Edmonton.

A quick lesson here: Never make decisions based upon guilt.

After a three-and-a-half-hour drive, we arrived in Alberta's capital. It was raining. As soon as we stopped for our first traffic light, the babies awoke and began howling.

There was considerable construction on the main road we were following, and so there were a lot of stops. Cars were backed up and sliding through the morass of mud that was seeping everywhere, which prompted our six-year-old to merrily explain to an increasingly grumpy driver just why the road was named Whitemud Avenue.

When we finally found the mall, we learned that the clearance to the underground parking was one inch lower than the height of our old blue van, and after backing out of one exit — much to the irritation of a few drivers following us — we tried another entrance, only to discover that it led to another ramp with the same clearance problem. With one look at the lineup behind us, my husband squared his shoulders and yelled, "I'm goin' in!"

We listened with acute annoyance as a heavy metal bar scraped over the roof of the van. Squeezed like tinned tuna below, we discovered two things:

One, the parking lot roof leaked very badly and streams of water were splashing down everywhere. There was more water down here than up above.

Two, on a rainy Saturday in July all tourists and many locals head for the same place. There was not one parking spot to be had.

It was the second roll bar across our rooftop as we exited the underground parking, with two babies howling and three children yelling, "Are we there yet? Can we get out now?" that prompted a frazzled Daddy to yell, "That's it! We're going home!"

This piece of news increased the howling chorus to five members.

Finally, at the far corner of an immense open parking lot, we found one spot. The dash for the nearest door, which – armed with a snugly and dragging a howling child or two – was not really a dash but a sort of quick limp, took long enough to soak everyone to the skin.

Once inside it was not better. Just different. Now we had to face thousands of shoppers, determined to see and do it all. There was a lot to see, and a lot to do.

We managed to lose only one child, whom we accidentally left at the top of an escalator (we could hear her screaming at the top as we were descending to the bottom), and to miss a rendezvous with some friends because we were standing, for forty-five minutes, at the wrong exit to the midway.

I think we only lost one parcel.

Nursing the babies while wearing a snugly, as thousands of people strolled by, was an interesting challenge, as was finding a place spacious enough to eat, and game enough, to fit and feed us all.

When we finally limped out six hours later and packed each child back into his and her particular car seat, the first thing they all said was,

"Gee, that was great! When do we start tomorrow?"

My husband gave me a long look, then turned to face the children and announced with an admirably sympathetic face, "I'm sorry kids, in Edmonton the malls are closed on Sundays."

A white lie on Whitemud. At the expense of our sanity, it was well spent.

1988:

Fall

Jane asked to come shopping with me today. This usually means they'll ask for a treat of some sort. Although I was ready for the question, it still caught me unprepared when she asked, "Mom, can we take a balloon ride and go to the moon? Pleeeease?"

Today they're sailing on a couch in the basement. "Look, Mom!" I strained to hear Alex with his head burried under a cushion. "This is where you steer the ship!"

"Ya!" echoed a muffled, enthusiastic Jane from under another cushion. "This is where you steal the fish!"

Greg's contribution to mixed vocabulary:

One of the kids, having raided the pots and pans cupboard walked through the house, banging pot lids together launched Greg into song:

> *"I'm gonna walk around with pots tonight*
> *Gonna walk walk walk till broad daylight..."*

Mai Tai's aren't drinks. They're what you can eat if you get close enough to Dad's chest.

And, in reference to Alex's horrible, stiff black socks: toxic "socks" syndrome.

Chapter 4

JUST ANOTHER THURSDAY

Breakfast time can be a good time for chewing and digesting. Chewing on what mom gives you and digesting the topic of the day.

One, there were two topics this morning. The first was whether or not Big Bird was a girl or a boy. Jane said girl, Charles said boy. Alex, our six-year-old, insisted that there was no way to actually tell with Big Bird, however Snuffy was a boy for sure.

From there we progressed to a topic dear to their hearts, and that was why they never got Fruit Loops or Sugar Crisp for breakfast. Everybody else (that is everybody on the TV commercials which, as a major part of our children's world, is everybody else) eats them. This was an old question, asked about once a week, and I delivered the same old answer as I delivered the same old bowl of porridge.

Alex gobbled his eat-it-because-it-is-nutritious cereal and raced off to catch the morning TV. I could hear the audience of six- and seven-year-olds responding enthusiastically to their cues from the game show that was playing. I knew that *Duck Tales*, his favourite show, was coming up next, and since he was allowed only one program in the morning, I considered advising him to turn the first show off. However, Stanley, his three-month-old brother who was beside me in his bounce chair, was yelling so hard that the advice would never have been heard. Stanley was yelling because Eddie was being nursed. Eddie was getting fed because he happened to be yelling louder than Stanley at the time (my method of deciding who got it first).

Our three-year-old, Jane who was just finishing her breakfast, suddenly gave an unholy "burp!" looked up in horror and said, "I'm going to throw up!"

There is nothing like those five words to galvanize a parent into action.

The nearest thing, which happened to be her brother Charles's almost empty bowl of porridge, was quickly pushed under her nose.

"Hey! That's my bowl!" was the immediate and indignant reaction from her brother.

"Yuck. I can't use that. It's dirrrrrty," said Jane.

"Gimme back my bowl!"

Baby still clutched to my breast, I rushed to the cupboard and grabbed a stainless steel bowl that I thought might work, and gave it to Jane, who discovered there were actually two bowls stuck together. A small diversion, but it was enough to make her forget about her stomach for the moment.

Charles asked to watch TV. "Sure," I said (rules verses sanity).

Stanley, momentarily quiet, resumed his howling with gusto.

Looking over, I noticed he was now sporting a steel

bowl on his head.

Jane and Charles had disappeared and so, it seemed, had Jane's momentary digestive distress.

I looked down at my bowl of cold porridge, then I looked at Eddie, still gnawing away. He looked at me and smiled. I smiled back, then leaned over and gently adjusted the bowl on howling Stanley's head so that it rode at a cocky angle.

Just another Thursday in the house.

Charles just strolled through the kitchen decked out with a snorkel and goggles. Alex is the golf ball and seems quite happy to roll by as he is smacked with a snorkel.

Chapter 5

FOOD GLORIOUS FOOD

Children have a way of taking grand notions and bringing them down to size.

Jane's idea of a black hole was a pitted olive.

***

I'd had an off day in the cooking department. Alex, eyeing my slightly charred grilled cheese sandwiches, said with a note of awe, "Gee, Mom, they look like they've been struck by lightning!"

That same night he found hope for my apple pie crust. "Well, you could use it as a Frisbee."

***

I fed the kids chocolate cake with spinach icing today. It was St. Patrick's Day after all, and something had to be green. The carcinogens in food colouring put that out of consideration, so I decided blended spinach slime was quite a satisfactory substitute.

Greg guessed it right away and wouldn't touch it. He amused himself by not telling the kids until they had finished eating the stuff. Alex did his swan-dive-throat-clutch that he was becoming more and more adept at — Mom got him again —but the middle two just laughed. The babies didn't care but they laughed too. They say laughter is good for digestion. Just they laughed too. They say laughter is good for digestion. Just don't do it when your mouth is full.

***

It's not that Jane didn't like food. One day I caught her embracing the fridge saying, "Oh fridgee fridgee fridgee, I love you!"

***

Seeing that Charles had nodded off at the supper table, a sympathetic Daddy gently scooped him up and took him to bed. His sister Jane, with a sideways glance at her untouched supper, said sadly in a tired voice, "I guess I'll go to bed too."

"Go ahead," I said, unmoved.

"Just a little sleep," she continued. "You can wake me when it's time for bezzert."

***

Eddie just cruised by, shedding copious quantities of crumbs and smelling faintly of cinnamon. Following his trail to the kitchen I stepped, barefoot, into a puddle of spilled juice and trod on a small pile of cheerios that crunched audibly beneath my foot. Muttering menacingly, I made my way to the pantry where my gummy feet were layered with a new concoction of nibbled crackers and a bag of spilled cinnamon.

When the mess was finally cleaned up and I was seated at the kitchen table, trying to read the paper, Stanley wobbled up and carefully placed a well chewed crust on my arm.

***

Charles was serenading his sister with his favourite cartoon theme song. She in turn was camped over her remaining mouthful of dinner, miserably pining for dessert and not at all impressed with her brother's efforts. It didn't help that he had already had a double helping of dessert.

"Stop it, Charles!" she finally yelled. "That singing makes me dance and then I choke on this stuff."

***

Stanley would always sit still and eat. However Eddie was another story. Having given up on trying to make him sit for a moment and eat, I decided to just put out a sandwich in the hope that he'd grab it on his way by. Stanley came through first, sporting a shirt, a sock and large pair of sunglasses.

After lapping Stanley a few times as he flew around the house, Eddie finally looked up and noticed the sandwich. Next time he flew through, it was with a pair of scissors that he used to cut the sandwich into tiny pieces, then said, "Done, Mom", and in a blur, was gone.

Chapter 6

SECOND CHILDHOOD

On a recent trip into town I found myself seated in transit next to two well-dressed businessmen who were having a lively conversation. They were not discussing the latest stock market report, but rather the merits of disposable and cloth diapers, what Little Jason was using and the state of his bottom as a result.

Now that's progress.

It is always a relief to know that there are other adults out in the workplace whose world revolves around the same things yours does.

Having children is rather like being born again into a child's world. Co-workers point to tell-tale signs of this rebirth, clucking over previously smart tailored business-men whose pants are now creased and worn in the wrong places from scooting along the carpet after a chubby bottom, or business-women who display squashed plastic frog lapel pins that say "Mom". A businessman or woman's business, it seems, is now in two worlds.

The real cause for this second childhood, however, is due to reasons beyond one's control: Everything you have gets replaced.

My husband and I brush our hair in the morning with either Garfield or Mickey Mouse brushes, whichever we can find. I have no idea where ours went. They're probably somewhere at the bottom of the toy box.

Kermit the Frog toothpaste somehow landed in our bathroom. It doesn't taste half bad. The other day, as we were watching *Home Improvement* with the kids and absently flossing our teeth, neither of us even noticed that we were using bubble gum-flavoured dental floss.

It is quite normal to shower with blue soap in the shape of a hippo, normal to douse your hair with green shampoo that smells like popsicles, from a bottle shaped like Batman and normal to dry yourself with a towel bearing the picture of a frazzled-looking duck that reads "I've got an attitude".

Who even notices when they grab a bowl with little marching mice around it to put their cereal in first thing in the morning?

Our once discerning palates are now lingering over ABC pasta and chicken nuggets as we read *Fat Men From Space* because the newspaper got used for the hamster cage.

The cruncher comes when you're out with friends at a movie and realize that you would really rather be playing in the wave pool with the kids.

Yes, everything gets replaced. Adulthood becomes second childhood, and the longer the space between your eldest and youngest, the longer your childhood is going to be. Why, a person could be a child for twenty, twenty-five years!

Gee, I guess that means I get to tear down the water slide, yelling "Cowabunga!" at the top of my lungs for a few years yet.

You really haven't appreciated a quiet morning in bed until you've had a lot that weren't.

One morning I found myself sniffing cautiously and asking Greg, "Do you smell dill?"

Eddie then climbed in next to us with his blanket. Both were covered with the new jar of fresh honey we'd bought the prior week and a generous dusting of dill.

I'm not sure which is worse, the sticky, or the slimy.

Last week it had been the carton of peach yogurt that he had emptied with his paws, then wiped all over his pajamas before joining us in the morning.

Chapter 7

INJURIES

Our six-year-old accidentally walked into a wall one day. I heard the loud thump when she connected, so I knew that the ensuing shriek was legitimate. There are shrieks, and then there are shrieks.

Being a responsible parent means sorting the small time bumps from the big-time bruises. Injury, perjury or surgery?

Depending upon the severity of the problem, and the age of the complainants, there are different methods of treatment involved here.

When they come in yelling from the back yard, the first thing to ask is "Is there any blood?" This will establish whether or not you should worry.

Bumps and scratches on a two to six-year-old usually respond well to Mom's magic lips. The kiss of health. Too bad Medicare couldn't package the system. We'd save a lot of tax dollars.

Band-Aids also work, but be prepared to have one for every child. If one of them has a patch on the elbow, there will be a yard full of empathisers who need an elbow patch too.

While six- to twelve-year-olds do like the hugs and sympathy, they don't always like you to know that they like it, so you should be ready with backup treatment.

Teenagers like hugs, but not necessarily your hugs. They too can be treated with alternate methods.

The backup is simple and almost always fail – proof: the old oral treatment remedy. Food. Treats. Through many years of experience, I've found it works like a darn.

On our daughter's bump today, I used mom's popsicles packed with blended fruit, acidophilus and vitamin C. A criple could run a marathon after one of those.

Recovery was swift and dramatic. In about three seconds, shrieks turned to slurps as she and all the rest of her siblings and whatever neighbours were hanging around sucked on the popsicles. It is amazing what a little treat will do.

Now, does this not make one pause for reflection?

Treating injuries – physical or emotional – with treats could very well revolutionise our economic and political system. Our government need look no further for its budgeting solutions.

Think, for example, how many hours and taxpayer dollars could be saved in our Parliament alone. When the opposition party starts to howl, the Speaker of the House could just yell, "Cookie time!" and pass out the Oreos.

I'll bet we would get a lot more bills passed.

Also, for those of you who hate the violence in sports? When the boys are giving it to one another on the boards at the next hockey game, rather than making the referee risk personal injury by breaking them apart, just have him toss in a few Kit Kats.

He must be sure, however, that there are as many bars as there are players or it could really turn ugly. Why, you could effectively protect yourself when you ride the city transit by just having a box of sweets in your bag. When the lad waves his weapon at you, toss him a Ding Dong.

I believe this could lower our crime rate and, through increased sales to the local general store, stimulate the economy.

Just what do you think brightens your sickly aunt's eye as she lies, supine, in that hospital bed? Is it the nurse with the foot-long needle? No! It is her beloved niece with a bag of jelly doughnuts!

I'm not saying the idea is perfect, but it is worth a try. When our son limped, howling, into the kitchen, clutching what we refer to as a sidewalk knee, I gave him the old magic kiss, hugged him and said very kindly, "There now, is that better?"

"Nope. Still hurts," came the teary reply, followed by, "Got any of those brownies left?"

Chapter 8

BRINGING HOME BABY(S)

When we left the hospital with our first-born son, I recall seeing a look of panic in my husband's eyes when the nurse handed him the baby carrier. We had previously taken about a half hour to secure the baby in it, checking and double checking that we had every strap and buckle in place. However, the thought of actually driving away with that precious, vulnerable package in it was more than either of us had prepared ourselves for. I remember driving at a very slow speed with our flashers on.

Three years later our first set of twins were tied in beside their older brother, who took his job very seriously. He sat between them in the car on the way home and poked them now and then to ensure that they were still alive.

Although we were hesitant to give our lad a baby to hold, he proved to be cautious and competent. He was also the best help a mother could have.

The twins, for their part, were even better entertainment for their older brother than TV. He was fascinated with every moving part of them. One day, after watching a couple of chubby little arms swinging through the air, he demanded, "Why do babies wear elastics on their wrists?"

When, three years later, the second set of twins arrived, Greg, looking a bit frazzled, brought the other three to the hospital for a visit. They were very pleased to find that the newborns had brought them gifts. I suppose it seemed logical, noting mom's girth before birth, that there would also be presents in there along with the babes. The children peered into each little tightly wrapped bundle to have a good look at the two wee boys we'd named Stanley and Eddie.

Unlike many, I loved being in the hospital. What's not to like? You're given three meals a day and snacks whenever you want them, you can stay in bed and read all day, and well-qualified personnel look after the babies when you're tired!

Though I'd politely asked if I could stay a week, I was given the door after just a couple of days.

Greg arrived looking even more shredded, but once we left the hospital doors, he'd perked up considerably and was actually humming as he plunked us all down in the car and whisked us home at a pace far, far different from the one set a mere five years ago.

Upon arrival I could see the three older siblings lined up at the window, noses pressed to the glass. When we came in the door, there was a scurrying about as Jane and Charles plunked down on the couch and looked up expectantly. When I bent to give one of the babies to Jane, she held up her hand and said, "Who's this?"

I peeked into the blanket to double check. "Eddie," I said.

"Nope. That's his," she said, pointing to her twin brother.

Apparently the claims had already been struck.

The ensuing weeks and months – and years – were busy alright, but having two sets of twins does not make one's life as crazy as one might think, for the first set is fascinated with the second. Each set entertains the other. And their older brother keeps busy with both.

The fascination continued as the older siblings took turns checking the progress of the new additions. One day Jane demanded, "Why do babies have pink teef?"

The thought of a new tooth took me by surprise, so I bent over and lifted a little lip. A set of pink of gums grinned back at me.

"Oh, babies don't have teeth" I explained.

"What? No teef?"

With a look of dismay, she ran off to advise her brother of the missing body part. The two of them returned moments later.

"Take 'em back. They need teef!"

Apparently he was still thinking about those absent teeth, for a few days later Charles asked,

"Mom, do babies have sharp gums?"

"No, why?"

"Eddie won't hurt me if he bites my leg, right?"

"Uh, right," I said.

A few minutes later Alex announced in a disgusted voice, "Ugh, Mom! Eddie is sucking on Charles's toes!"

It's a wonder kids survive their childhood.

In five years you might say that our cautious behaviour abated somewhat. I have a mathematical theory for this, which does not stand up well to scrutiny. However, I developed it to keep a measure of sanity in my life.

Let's say that there is a finite amount of caution and worry that a person can have. If you have one child, you can really smother him or her in it. If you have five or six children, then you have to spread that a little thinner, so that they all get a bit.

One interesting side effect this thinly doled caution had was that our eldest son began to fill in when my concern seemed a wee bit lacking. For example, he might become a bit frazzled when set number one would have "car" races with set number two. The cars consisted of the bucket seats that we transported the babies in. Set number one would lap the house, lurching precariously around corners. The faster they went, the more the babies giggled.

Of course there is only so much stress a seven-year-old can harbour, and after a time he would give up and just join in the fray. The cat hated this, particularly when they would trap him and push him around too, in whatever mode of transport they could scrounge; usually it was the roasting pan. That way all three could race.

A couple of years later, contrary to dire warnings from our doctor that there was something like a 75 percent chance that I would have multiples again, we decided that our lone daughter needed female companionship. I figured that I'd had a singleton once, so I could do it again. After all, when you're wet, what's another raindrop?

When we announced that number six was on the way, we got a variety of reactions. The youngest set of twins just nodded as if to say, "Sure, sign 'em up". The eldest set laughed. Great – more chaos! Our number-one son slapped his forehead and groaned.

"Mom, Dad, please tell me you're kidding."

Perhaps my mathematical theory didn't work for everyone. He seemed a bit stressed.

Shortly thereafter, we brought home one little girl to make an even half dozen.

When we arrived at the house, there were five very eager pairs of arms waiting to enfold her. The youngest two plunked themselves onto the couch, breathless. When I handed her to one of them, the other looked at me blankly.

"Where's mine?"

When we explained that there was only one this time, his twin brother said, "Well, go back and get another one!"

I'd been reasoning with youngsters for long enough to understand their minds by now: perhaps you could get 'teef' and babies from same place.

Unfortunately, that factory only manufactures by the half dozen. It's now closed for renovation.

Chapter 9

DINNER TIME

It was Friday, Dad was late, and was kids' day, which meant they got to select the menu. Not surprisingly, it was spaghetti. This was easy to make, they liked it – I didn't complain. The babies, however, rated a little extra nutrition. Besides, they were young and would usually eat what they were given.

As I was peeling their avocado, Eddie, whom I had placed too close to the table, crawled over his high chair and onto the table, much to the delight of the other four. When he put his hand smack into one of their spaghetti-strewn plates, their delight knew no bounds.

I put him back, tied him down with his high chair belt, my apron, and a rope from the closet, and delivered the avocado. His brother Stanley began eating his. Eddie investigated his avocado's green interior.

Turning my back for a moment, I whipped up a sensible, sneaky dessert, mixing tofu, yogurt and my strawberry preserves together. The kids would get that protein and calcium if the cook had her way.

My happy humming and stirring was cut short as I responded to a wild cry from the direction of the floor. Seven-year-old Alex – for some reason on his hands and knees under the babies' high chairs – was clutching his head and bellowing. In answer to my querying look, he uttered a strangled, "I've been slimed!"

Above him was the little *slimer*, Eddie, peering over the edge of his high chair with gaping, giggling lips just oozing avocado. This of course caused an exodus from the table as the four-year-old twins crowded under the high chairs with the perverted hope that they too would be slimed. Shooing the reluctant would-be *slimees* back to their places, I looked over to find that Eddie had magically finished most of his avocado. I was surprised and checked the floor. It was awful, but among the mess of spaghetti, crackers and unidentified food objects, there was no avocado.

"Good boy!" I praised. He smiled a very green smile and waved an equally green and slimy hand. Stanley meanwhile was trying to reach his sister's spaghetti and was yelling very loudly, so he was given some. He did, after all, eat the avocado.

A one-year-old does interesting things with a strand of spaghetti. It is held across the nose, over the head, and finally bitten in the middle.

Alex, who had his dessert now, offered to demonstrate how eating pudding can be, if done properly, just like listening to a machine gun. The yogurt-tofu proved to be a hit, with seconds all around. My joy was only mildly curtailed by the sight of Eddie standing up in his chair like a gopher, having Samson-like snapped all his chains. He was covered now with avocado and pudding and was trying hard to imitate his older brother's machine gun rendition. He succeeded in covering his twin with a fine green and white spray, which settled around Stanley's little spaghetti goatee.

Unwilling to transport either of them over the carpet to the bathroom tub in that condition, I stripped them on the spot. And found the missing avocado. It was tucked securely in Eddie' pants.

One should not put their child on the counter when they are at the bank. This is not for safety reasons.

Today it was Charles who was fussing after waiting for the long line of customers to be served, so as Jane waited patiently by my legs, I perched her brother up beside me. Unbeknownst to me, he had begun to explore the nether regions of his nose. I heard a few muffled snickers from the line behind as he turned to me and, finger dangling in my face, said quite loudly, "Here mom. What do I do with this?"

The other night when I staggered back to bed after nursing the twins, I was annoyed to find that Greg had taken my pillow. I tried to get it back, but he had it in a death grip. Undaunted, and noticing he was still asleep I pulled and elbowed with a fierce determination, only to have him mumble in his sleep, "We're sharing, not fighting."

Chapter 10

POODLES, PICKLES AND PIMPLES

I can't imagine a farm without a dog. In fact, I don't think I know of any farms without one. They are man's, and most particularly, children's best friend. Our shepherd is no exception, accepting hugs, wrestling and leftovers with equal enthusiasm.

One Saturday afternoon several years ago, when I was driving my children home in our van, we pulled alongside a pickup truck that had a dog in the back of it. The babies responded with enthusiastic "woof-woofs".

The other three had a stirring discussion as to what breed of dog it was. After dismissing bulldog, sheep dog, poodle and wolf, they finally decided that it looked more like a pig and therefore, quite logically it seemed, was likely a pit bull terrier. That is, Alex, the seven-year-old said it was a pit bull. Four-year-old Charles called it a pickle terrier; his sister Jane, a pimple terrier. In any case, it was very dangerous.

The appearance of the pickle, or rather pimple, launched some interesting stories.

Jane, her eyes wide and bright said in a hushed voice,

"There were a couple of guys sitting on a bench? And a pimple terrier walks up? And bites off their legs!"

Alex was unmoved.

"Oh ya? Where did you hear that?"

"On the news," was the quick reply.

This seemed at least to satisfy her twin brother. Entering into the spirit of the discussion, he launched the following.

"Well, there was this guy who was just sittin' there and this pickle terrier came up and ate off all his skin and just left his brain and his bones."

This appeared to raise some doubt in his listeners, for Jane asked, "Nothin' but his brain and his bones?"

"And his shoes," said Charles after some thought, at once making the story believable. To his sister, that is. His older brother remained unconvinced.

"Oh ya? Where did you see that? On the news?" "Nope," he replied, not missing a beat. "On video."

"Oooo, gross!" squealed a delighted Jane.

This sparked a heated discussion of the grossest things they had ever seen on video, television, and at the movies. The possibilities were endless.

There was a green-faced, warty boogey man who boogedy-ized someone's mother, and giant were chickens who pecked people and turned them into feathered, crazed, clucking were people. Eating live beetles or eyeball soup ranked highly. But the clincher came from Charles who, with a screwed-up nose and a look of utter disgust on his face, recounted an episode he had seen on television.

"There was this guy and he saved this lady. And she turned around and kissed him. Yuck!"

"Oh, too gross."

For once his older brother was on his side. Jane just giggled. Bizarre tales can make you do that.

Today the kids' current TV favourite, Ghost Busters, is featuring were-chickens (as opposed to werewolves). The children alternate between watching the TV and hiding behind the couch, occasionally popping up to take a peek at who is being zapped or slimed or turned into a were-chicken next. After the show, they spent a wild morning racing around the house yelling, "There's ghosts in there!" Jane, finally collapsed at the breakfast table, looked down and announced, "There's a ghost in my toast."

The kids have found a new way to torment one another. They put Eddie in their sibling's room and quickly shut the door. Eddie can cause more havoc in a room than a weasel in a chicken coop. The beauty of the trick is that when the inevitable yelling from the older sibling ensues and Mom storms in, Eddie can't be blamed because he's "just a baby".

1989:

Spring

Jane marched into the living room today, complaining that Charles wouldn't play house with her. I asked her, "Who do you want to be?"

"The mom," she said, hands on hips. So far so good.

"Charles," I asked, "why not play house? You'd make a good Dad. Or brother," I added when he rolled his eyes.

"No!" explained his sister. "I want him to be Spike the dog."

When a child is very quiet, it is time to check on what they are doing, so when Jane and her pal Claire had been in her room for a while, I thought I'd just check to see what was up. There was a giggle and a scuffle when I arrived. It took me a minute to notice that there were a lot of bald Barbie dolls on the floor, and a minute more to notice that Jane looked decidedly different. Half her hair was missing – the left half. Panicked and with visions of sending a small severely trimmed Barbie home, I asked Claire, who had a lovely long ponytail, to turn around. And there it was, swinging just above the scissors in her hands, still lovely and long. I didn't know whether to laugh or cry. In answer to my query, Claire said sweetly, "I did a nice job of Jane's I know, but I'd never let her fix my hair."

Jane's remained 'fixed' for a few months. After all, as her father always said, "the difference between a good and a bad haircut is just a matter of time".

Greg took the kids to the lake. As they played he tried his hand at fishing. He looked quite exhausted when he got home and, looking over at me, said, "The only bite I got all afternoon was when Stanley bit my leg."

May

Alex and Greg just arrived at the door from their fishing

expedition at Lake Bonavista, and yes, Alex caught a trout. A lovely two-pounder. Both father and son were happy and excitedly recounted the story of how they tried and tried to no avail, and how finally as they were coming in, Alex found an old marshmallow in the boat, used it and presto!

When Alex finally wandered off, Greg confided, "Hon, he was sooooo excited," and proceeded to explain how they had smashed into another boat in the great fight with the fish, and how the trout swam under the docks before they finally got it into the boat.

Later that evening, Alex, with a confidential gleam in his eye came quietly into the kitchen when I was alone and said, "Mom. Dad was sooooo excited…"

Winter

Jane offered to babysit today. All went well with solemn little Stanley seated on the couch until his mobile twin cruised up and smacked him on the head with an eggbeater. Stanley started to howl, so Jane started to sing, which is her method of cheering everyone up. Stanley, however, was crying so hard that she had to sing very loudly. Leaning over him with fixed determination, she belted out "Jingle Bells", which happens to be the happiest song she knows.

Could have been the hollering, could have been the singing, but soon Eddie lent his lungs to the fray.

Two against one can be a problem and Jane is no fool. Above the din, there was a "Charles! I need help in here!"

Charles, sensing chaos, came happily and joined with Jane in the chorus....

"Oh, what fun it is to cry…"

"On a one house oooooo-pen sleigh," they hollered merrily in stereo, as the babes, also in stereo, hollered with distinctly less enthusiasm.

I guess this was what one would call quadraphonic sound. Unfortunately, there's never that dial to switch it off...

Chapter 11

IT'S POTTY TIME

There are certain mileposts in a child's life that mark a transition from one developmental stage to another. Just when they are reached is often a point of pride with parents.

When it came to toilet training, I considered myself to be very clever in having "trained" three children to use the potty in a fairly short period of time when they were around two years old.

Whenever I consider myself to be clever, life kindly helps me regain a sense of reality. In this case, it was twin boys: Stanley and Eddie.

When they were two I began the training. These two did not respond to the usual bribes of favourite food, stickers, stamps, or praise – or threats and guilt for that matter. Six months later their baby sister arrived and they adopted a more philosophical stance: If I didn't get mad at their sister, then why did I get mad at them when they used a diaper?

I limped along with my efforts, muttering as I changed three bottoms, and comforting myself from time to time with the thought that surely when they were teens the diapers would not fit under skin-tight jeans.

It all came to a head one sunny summer day when they

were three years old. I plunked Eddie down on the toilet seat, and growled through gritted teeth, "You don't get off till you put something in."

He responded by putting his little nose in the air and saying, "I will nevah, nevah use the potty."

I looked into his eyes, and it was then that I knew he was right. I would nevah, nevah be out of diapers. I would be up to my elbows in it forever. They would be climbing on the old yellow school bus with a sandwich and a diaper in their backpacks, and the school nurse would be calling me in for counseling.

Admitting defeat gave me an unexpected sense of clarity. What if, I reasoned, I just didn't put diapers on them? What if I got rid of their pants, and just gave them a tee shirt each day? It was summer-time. Who was going to see them in the back yard anyway? At least then I wouldn't have to change diapers! With a sudden lift of the heart, I hoisted Eddie off the toilet, pulled off his shorts and said, "Off you go then."

He looked at me blankly. Where was the rest of the outfit? I explained that from now on, he didn't have to wear anything except a shirt, and by the way, call Stanley in because the same went for him.

The two of them reveled in their newfound freedom. They leaped around the yard and rolled in the grass like a couple of puppies. Their siblings were a bit baffled, but had long resigned themselves to never attempt to understand a mother's mind. *So now we can go naked. Mom's off her rocker again.*

As a matter of fact, I was happily rocking in my rocker when Stanley showed up and said he had to pee. I told him to use the bushes. With a shocked look, he ran back out and advised Eddie of the new plan. This brought them both back in, hands on hips.

"Well, I have to poo!" Eddie fired at me.

I smiled kindly and told him to use the bushes.

"I can't use the bushes, they're prickly. Gimme back my diaper!" was his angry response.

I shook my head sadly. "Well, you've got no pants, and no diaper anymore. It is either the bushes or the potty".

Sometimes, desperation can be the mother of invention. And desperate mothers are nothing if not inventive.

They nevah used a diaper again.

Asked by their Auntie Kit if the three eldest would like to go to Burger King for supper, Charles replied, "No. Because there's probably kings in there and kings fight."

Chapter 12

JAM TOE

When you've been married to a person for a long time, you think you know everything there is to know about them. However, there is a side of them that only reveals itself when you have children. It is then that your spouse's childhood quirks resurface, and it is then, I might add, that some of their unusual behavior patterns that you have always wondered about begin to make sense.

Take, for example, toe jam. My husband has always paid particular attention to his feet, fussing over them and taking time to ensure that each little toenail is nicely trimmed.

One evening, I overheard him conversing with then three-year-old Eddie and Stanley. The three of them were huddled over Stanley's toes, deep in a serious conversation.

"This," explained their dad as he carefully spread Stanley's toes wide, "is toe jam."

Puzzled, I peered over to find out what they were talking about. My husband was pointing to the bit of fluff and dirt that was parked between two little pink toes. Below me, two small heads bent forward to have a good look at the offending material.

"You need to make sure that you get all that stuff out from between your toes each time you have a bath," added my husband.

Because I'd safely navigated my life without checking between my toes each time I had a shower, I didn't give much credence to their father's advice. Turns out I should have.

Young Stanley took his father's suggestion to heart – or rather, foot. Any time he could catch his siblings when they were stationary for more than a minute, Stanley would pull off their shoes and examine their toes. His older siblings thought this was great fun, and would lie back on the couch as they were watching cartoons and just let Stanley poke away between their toes. If he missed anyone, they would call him over.

"Hey Stan, check out this one. I haven't had a bath in a week."

Whenever we went anywhere in the van, he and his brother pulled off their shoes and socks to check for toe jam. I'd tear off to an appointment, only to arrive and find two sets of pink toes wiggling at me – or three if they could get their hands on their baby sister. As I muttered away on my hands and knees, searching for lost socks and shoes, they would gaze at me, baffled by my frustration and just say, "Jam toe!"

No amount of coaxing or threatening could quell their enthusiasm. I tried putting elastics around their ankles, and when that didn't slow them down, I tied great granny knots in their laces. The kids had Houdini feet – they could slip out of anything.

When he heard about the situation in the back seat, my husband thought that it was quite funny, until it happened to him one day when he was in a hurry.

He wheeled up to his destination, ripped open the side door of the van, and discovered that all six of our kids had whipped off their shoes. Searching and then sorting to figure out whose foot each shoe belonged to took about five minutes, which was four minutes longer than his patience lasted.

He returned home, exasperated, and finished recounting the day's adventure by saying, "They're all nuts!"

I had little sympathy for this evildoer who created the foot fetish in the first place.

"Wrong food group," I said darkly. "Not nuts. Fruit. Jam to be exact."

Charles has been walking stiff-legged around the house for the past few days, saying in a singsong voice, "I hear and obey. I hear and obey."

Who says T.V. isn't a positive influence.

Chapter 13

BEETS

I have an old Russian book on herbal remedies that tells of an application of beets and yogurt on the face that gives one a youthful blush. My mother is Ukrainian, and it goes without saying that beets were a common part of our diet. I did try the stuff on my cheeks and turned pink all right. I think it was due to an allergic reaction.

My sisters and I tolerated beet borscht, but we were not keen on boiled beets. I remember my exasperated father looming large over us as we poked at them on our plates, yelling, "Just eat your beets!"

Mom never wasted any part of the beet. If we wouldn't eat the root, then we would eat the leaf, and this we did quite enthusiastically, after carefully wrapping them around a small finger of dough to make what we called dog bones. One simply baked them, smothered them in fresh dill and onions fried in butter, and dipped them in sour cream. You couldn't even taste the leaf.

My children loved these dog bones (although we had the neighbours wondering what the heck were feeding our children); however, when they were young, like their mother and aunties before them, they were not keen on the beets themselves.

One day when I had cooked a batch of beets for my husband and myself I noticed that the water left over was a deep, inviting shade of purple. Rather like grape juice.

An idea was born.

Everyone knows that vegetable water is packed with vitamins and minerals. I just put a bit of sugar in the beet juice, added some vitamin C crystals (I figured that C gets destroyed by the heat) and made popsicles.

It might have worked, except Greg, for the first time ever, decided to have a popsicle with the kids. I guess the purple shade was more inviting than I thought.

While our four-year-old twins slurped and gobbled happily, my husband slowly looked up from his frozen treat and said, "Okay. This isn't grape juice."

"Right."

"So what is it?" he demanded.

I hedged, hoping he'd eat more.

"Does it taste good?"

"It tastes…different. What did you put in there?"

"Beets," I replied calmly.

"Right, hon. Tell me. I need to know."

My husband quit there and then.

Seven-year-old Alex, who had been listening intently, made an admirable swan dive, clutching his throat and landing upon the floor, purple popsicle at his side. The twins slurped their way right to the last drop, which made me at least feel justified.

I presented my case to my husband. They tasted fine. They were packed with healthy stuff and were completely organic.

His defense?

"Next thing you know you'll be feeding us Brussels sprout cake with cabbage icing. No. I will not eat them – on principal."

When children grow up their tastes don't change. Their excuses get more sophisticated.

Just eat your beets.

Eddie has been repeating the same thing lately, and it lifts my spirits like nothing else:

"Mom, I have some very good news for ya... I love you."

Chapter 14

FIRST SKATES

If you were raised in Canada, you probably spent a lot of time on the local pond or arena, bashing away at pucks. Hockey is a great sport. It gives kids – and parents – something to do in those long winter months. For some with very talented kids, it can be every long month of the year.

If you are a Canadian father, it is winter time, you're really tired of arenas and believe that the kids have been watching far too much TV and need to get out in the fresh air, a clever thing to do is to flood the back yard and make your own rink.

Making your own rink is actually easier said than done. It took my husband days to figure out how to contain the water, and days more to make the surface somewhat smooth. However, he was determined to give the kids some exercise and get them out of their mother's hair. Getting out of your mother's hair can be quite a tangle if you are only four years old.

The morning I took Stanley and Eddie for their first outing on Dad's new rink, it took half an hour to find their bob skates, which were in the shed. Unfortunately, only three made it through from the previous season. It took another half hour to get the two suited, booted, mittened and toqued, and to quell the fight about who was going to get two skates and who would get only one.

Eddie (who got the pair) was first out on the ice. Eyes flashing, body taut and ready, he stood poised at the edge of the ice for about half a minute, then looked first at his skates and then at me.

"They don't work!" he said, with a mixture of shock and dismay.

"They don't?" I asked.

"No. They don't work," he repeated.

I bent down to examine the skates, looked at him blankly and said, "Sure they do."

"No they don't," he repeated firmly. "Look at 'em – they don't skate!"

I explained that in order for them to work, he had to move his feet around. This he did, somewhat doubtfully, then announced that all he was doing was walking around. After about three minutes of this, he turned and headed for the house, passing his brother Stanley, who had finally limped up to the ice on one bob skate.

"They don't even work, Stanley," Eddie tossed over his shoulder in disgust.

Stanley stepped out on the ice, his skate-shod limb shot out from under him and he landed flat on his bottom. I could just barely hear Eddie over Stanley's loud wailing, yell, "I told ya they didn't work!"

When he could finally speak, Stanley glared at me accusingly.

"That ice is slippery, Mom."

With no further explanation deemed necessary, he too turned and limped back into the house.

A half hour later they were de-toqued and de-mittened and pacified with hot chocolate and a cookie.

It was only a matter of minutes later that Eddie proclaimed, "There's nothin' to do mom"

I paused for a moment, then offered, "I wonder what's on TV."

Greg has just cornered all the kids and herded them into the bathroom. It's that favourite time at the end of the day when they all get to pile in and splash. At least Greg is approaching this with a smile and a song. I can hear him in there, amid the shrieks, singing loudly and quite off key an old Waylon Jennings tune:

"Oh, throw another babe in the tubby…"

Chapter 15

GICK

When you are a family of eight – and six of them happen to be under the age of eight – a vacation becomes less "where will we go this year?" and more "so honey, define vacation".

When our youngest was a year old, the definition became family camp on Quadra Island, which was definitely fun for us all and our home away from home for many years. It was, however, a seventeen hour drive from our home, so we usually tried to make the trip in two days. This particular year Greg flew home to get back to work, but it was the summer and the kids weren't ready to end the vacation. A good friend unexpectedly offered us her vacant home in British Columbia's lovely Okanagan and my niece very kindly agreed to travel with the gang, so it was decided that we'd pause in Vernon on our way home. Incredibly, the only stipulation of our free residency was that we did not let the cat out.

One cannot vacation in the Okanagan without visiting their lakes, so one very hot day we packed up the kids and went to the wonderfully clear and warm Kalamalka Lake for a picnic and a swim. After spreading out numerous towels, blankets, sand digging tools, life jackets, inflatable toys, food and beverages, we noticed that the baby was in dire need of a diaper change. Unfortunately, I had left the diaper bag behind. She was quite happy to be bare and carefree, but we thought it prudent to fetch something, just in case. This was, after all, a public beach. Telling a noticeably nervous niece that I would be back in a flash, I jumped in our very hot old blue ford van and drove back to our residence.

I opened the door and let myself in very carefully, in case the cat should be lurking nearby, ready to bolt. Kicking off my sandals, I headed for the basement, where the diaper bag was. The power was out for some reason, and I had to grope around in the dark. Unfortunately, the cat was hiding down there, and as I cautiously felt my way around a corner, I trod upon it. We both jumped and screeched. I ran into a wall, the kitty ran upstairs. Following to be sure it was not terminally injured, I cornered it in a second-floor bedroom. As I lunged to grab it, we both discovered that the window where it was cowering was open. It slipped through.

With only one thought in mind, and that was the single stipulation regarding our free residency in this home, I sized up the window and decided if pussy jumped out, there must be something to jump on. I crawled through, hot on its trail. And its trail was indeed very hot.

The window gave way to the flat tar-and-sand-roofed carport which, when trod upon bare-footed, was agony. At least for me. The cat did not seem to mind at all, for it was sitting at the edge of the roof, calmly cleaning its coat. Cursing audibly, I began hopping toward it, but paused mid–step when the neighbor next door came out and walked toward her car. Thinking that a stranger standing upon the neighbor's roof beside an open window might look a bit suspicious, I remained motionless, save for the lifting and shifting of my feet, which along with the rest of my body, were beginning to turn a bright pink. Flamingo-like, I waited up there, one eye on the cat, one eye on the woman, willing her not to look up; willing her even more vehemently to get in her car and leave.

After fussing endlessly with her keys, the woman finally climbed in her car. As she did so, the cat stretched languidly, then to my horror, leaped over the edge of the roof. When the car was gone, I hobbled to the carport edge, and looked over.

The cat, it appeared, had not suicided itself, but had hopped down upon the roof of my Ford, and thence to the ground below. Thinking that anywhere was better than the burning tar, I too lowered myself to the van's roof, only to discover two things: hot metal is hotter than hot tar, and infinitely more flexible than a roof top.

The ground was not more flexible, but was definitely cooler, which compensated for the thud that was felt throughout my body upon contact.

I found the cat cowering behind a very prickly rosebush, and after tangling my hair and shirt on the bush, I was finally able to nab it.

Feline firmly tucked under my arm, I marched to the front door, only to find that I had inadvertently locked it behind me when I had first entered.

Retracing my steps was a very painful process, particularly climbing up on the van roof with a very nervous feline in my arms. The cat hissed at me and – such was my mood – I hissed right back. This seemed to subdue it somewhat, at least until I was able to stuff it back in the window. It bolted out of sight, and I never did see it again for the duration of our stay.

The children, and particularly their cousin were very happy to see me when I returned to the beach. The latter lifted a wailing baby and advised me that she thought the wee one was possibly not feeling well. This the baby confirmed with one word: "gick!"

And gick she did, all over my tattered shirt.

The children all cried when we told them that it was time to leave. After picking up various towels, blankets, sand digging tools, life jackets, inflatable toys, food and beverages – and the diaper bag – we climbed into our very hot van. They then cried even harder because the smell of gick on their mom's shirt was more than anyone could bear.

We left early the next day. The kids weren't that keen on returning to dull old summer on the farm, but dull can be pretty attractive when it comes to a vacation with the pack.

1991:

Summer

As we headed down to campfire one evening at our summer camp at Homewood on Quadra Island two of the male counselors scooped up our four-year-olds and put them on their shoulders. As the lads jogged along merrily, one of the counselors casually asked, "Eddie, what are you rubbing in my hair?"

"Oh, just a boogi," he said breezily.

Responding to the shrieks from the female counselors, he added, "Ju-ust kidding."

We took a short vacation once to see our friends in Seattle. They are very brave friends, for they agreed to have all of us there for a weekend. We left from Vancouver, Canada, and the closer we got to our destination, the more restless the kids became. Stanley kept asking the same question over and over:

"Where are we going?"

His older siblings repeated over and over the same answer, "To Seattle!"

Finally the poor little chap yelled, "Who's Attle?"

To celebrate Easter, the mall set up a little corral where children were allowed to play with chicks, bunnies and baby goats. The kids had a ball. They petted the bunnies and Charles got a chance to pick up one of the fuzzy yellow chicks. He held it carefully in his hands, his face a picture of joy.

That evening Jane announced to a startled Daddy that Charles had picked up some chicks that day.

"Oh? Where?" he asked.

"At the mall" she replied.

Greg, puzzled and faintly, amused, asked, "How?"

With a look of forced patience, Charles replied, "By their feet, Dad."

Looking at me, Greg shrugged. "I guess they do it differently these days."

"Ya, and I petted some bunnies too," Charles added proudly.

His Dad paused, carefully stroked his chin then said, "I think I'll go hang out at the mall."

We have a mouse in the storage pantry. A SMART mouse. He's been having a ball in there and has either sprung or avoided every trap that I've set. When the kids got wind of the situation, they invited the whole neighborhood over for tours. When it was her turn, Jane donned a hard hat and boots and carried a wooden gun before entering and giving the all - clear to her pals.

Chapter 16

BOWLING

I took the kids bowling today. Greg was at work, and our church group had planned a family day at the lanes long ago, so thinking it might be entertaining for the kids, we set out.

Note to self: Kids don't need any extra entertaining. Life for them is simply a mad scramble of endless entertainment.

Before we actually started the games, the other family groups suggested that we have a little warm-up. Let the kids throw a few balls just to get the feel of it.

We got the feel pretty quickly.

Eddie felt that a good way to deliver the ball was to drop it and kick it. I've never seen a ball creep up on a pin. Contact came just as the ball ran out of steam. The pin leaned back, and then righted itself, the ball resting at its side.

Stanley felt that a better way was to push it with all his might. One after another, balls made it about half way up and stopped in the gutter.

Charles threw a magnificent ball that arrived just as Jane flipped the reload button and the sweep bar dropped down. The ball hit it and ricocheted back down the alley.

Alex felt that he would get a better chance of hitting the pins if he swung the ball a few times between his legs first. Unfortunately, he let go at the wrong end of the swing and the ball flew back past some very startled players and crashed into the seats.

As this was happening, Stanley and Eddie, running out of balls due to the fact that most of them were half way up the gutter, hopped from lane to lane collecting balls.

The warm-up lasted ten minutes, after which it occurred to me that perhaps the folks who ran the alley might be open to giving me my money back. Our church group was very sympathetic, but no one – including the owners of the alley – tried to stop us from leaving. The only ones showing any regret were the children, who left with a howl and a wail and four balls lined up in the gutter. I took that as a sign that one day they would return to the lanes. One day in the future. By themselves.

1991:
November

I noticed our one-year-old Elly open the cupboard and begin rooting through. As I watched, she came upon a cookie box, opened it, leaned back and gave it an enthusiastic, "Hi!"

1992:
January

We were chatting about Shakespeare the other day, and I launched into those famous "to be or not to be" lines that I remembered from Hamlet's soliloquy.

Dad turned to his ten-year-old son and said, "I'll bet you don't even know who wrote that."

"Sure I do. It's William Armstrong.

"Close. William Shakespeare"

"Oh ya. I know that guy," Alex said breezily. "He wrote Mario and Juliet."

Charles came home from school today and announced, "Hey! Kelsey threw up at school today!"

The tragedy drew swift, enthusiastic reaction from his siblings. "All over herself?" squealed Jane, thinking of the worst possible scenario.

"Nope"

"On her math book?" piped up a hopeful Alex, whose ideal spot was somewhere different.

"Nope," gleamed Charles. "On her lunch!"

"Gross!" came the delighted chorus.

Detecting comedy in tragedy is an art form kids have mastered.

Chapter 17

SIXTEEN CHICKENS ON A TRAMPOLINE

When we moved to the country, I had visions of sunny summers and green pastures; of walking out with a basket on my arm to collect warm brown eggs to feed my happy family.

Anticipating free food, Greg was happy to cooperate with the chicken part. I suggested three laying hens. He did a bit of research and learned that a significant percentage of chicks, which are shipped at a day old, die in transport. He ordered thirty. A couple of days later I received a desperate call from the post office asking if I could come in quickly to collect the chicks. It is amazing what comes in the mail these days. When I arrived, there they were in a box on the countertop, the loud cheep-cheeping providing entertainment for the surprised folks in the lineup.

It was a chilly April afternoon when I picked up the birds, and keeping in mind the warning about losing them in transport, I worried they'd die of hypothermia, if not of bumping and colliding en route. So I put a seat belt around the box, jacked up the heat in the van and tried to drive very carefully. I put some music on, choosing carefully for something soothing. I hoped it wasn't a sinister portent when "Jamaica Farewell" started to play. They got awfully quiet on the way home, and I figured for sure I'd killed half of them, but when I arrived, they were still shuffling around.

The arrival of the chicks coincided with our younger set of twins' third birthday, and they and the rest of their siblings decided that the fuzzy little guys were just the most amazing birthday present ever. The chicks were held, petted, kissed, decorated, wrapped, fed and fondled. Not one of the little critters died from the attention, which just goes to show you how tough chickens are.

"Hide The Chick" became the game of choice. One child would sneak a chick out of the box we had set up in the laundry room, and hide it. The rest would then go look for it, aided considerably by the bird, which would cheep-cheep in panic from under the couch or from inside a cupboard. Sometimes the kids would hide nine or ten at once and have a round up. Sometimes they would not all get rounded up, and Dad would find one snoozing in his shoe as he bolted out the door for work in the morning, causing panic for both the bird and the man at the other end of the shoe.

Chicks, we discovered, are cute for a week or two, then they start getting big – which is what we had hoped for – and smelly, which was what we had failed to consider. In a month the flies moved in and very shortly afterward the chicks moved out to an old coop in the yard that had, by the look of it, been there a long while. It cost ninety dollars for a heat lamp, feeder, water can, hay, chicken feed and, of course, the chicks themselves. So much for free food.

Even though the chickens finally vacated, the children

never quite shook the idea that these birds were their pets. They still visited the coop regularly, checking on the flock's progress.

On a sunny afternoon a month or so later, I was in our kitchen with a friend, when three-year-old Eddie came rolling in, elbows chugging like a little Popeye, and singing, "Yo-ho–ho, yo–ho-ho, sixteen chickens on a tram – po – yeeeeen. Yo-ho-ho".

Both my friend and I started to laugh, then at the same time stopped and stared at one another for one awful moment. We bolted out the back door, in the direction of the trampoline. There on the canvas were about a half dozen chickens clucking crazily, and beside them was Stanley, merrily bouncing them through the air, cheered on by his siblings and various neighbours.

As Stanley came down, the birds went up, cackling wildly. When Stanley went up, the birds bounced down, feathers flying.

How long this had been going on was uncertain, but if it didn't end soon, there would be a bunch of bald chickens in the hen house. True, they flapped gamely, but they were making little progress toward the edge of the trampoline.

Once we got Stanley off the canvas, we tried to catch the chickens, but they staggered around out of our reach for quite a while, apparently too dizzy to use their wings.

It took some time to round up the other two dozen panicked poultry that had been set free, particularly with the children and their friends in the chase. There were chickens and kids everywhere.

When the last bird was stuffed back into the hen house, and the last feather floated to the ground, the two little culprits flopped happily onto the trampoline upon which, most unfortunately, the chickens' calling cards had been dropped.

Chicken droppings are a nasty thing to get out of one's hair, but are – according to their older sister and brothers – quite the most hilarious thing to have to happen to a person.

No doubt the chickens agree.

Cartoons, in this case "Who Framed Roger Rabbit", have a direct influence on a child's vocabulary. Four-year-old Eddie managed some transgression that I figured needed discipline so as usual, he was sent to his room with Mom's admonition, "Get to your room, buddy."

Before leaving in a huff, he paused, turned, crossed his arms and fired back, "Don't call me buddy, toots."

1992:

June

In order to get them there without complaint, after church each Sunday I take the kids to McD's. Whatever works.

Today in the van on the way to McD's, Stanley called Jane a McBum. I admonished him saying that was not nice. A few minutes later, after some giggles and mumbles in the back seat, Eddie piped up, "I know what she is – McToots!"

It's been a nightmare around here. Greg decided that all the kids needed to learn to defend themselves, so he's enrolled them in karate. Every time I turn around, there is a "Hi – ya!" and a foot appears an inch from my nose. Guess I should've enrolled myself.

1993:

February

The boys just came down with the chicken pox today. They were very itchy and had been trying hard not to scratch. As a diversion, I produced a new stamp set I'd set aside for just such an emergency as this. On the stamps were the alphabet and various animals.

For a time, the diversion seemed to work. Stanley found the letter X and, happily stamping it on his paper announced, "Hey! I did an X."

Busy with something in the kitchen, Greg casually replied, "X marks the spot."

Stanley, his fingers twitching longingly near his itchy eyebrow, said very sadly, "Don't wemind me."

My sister Judy called today, and as we were on the phone, Alex walked up, shirtless and with a half-embarrassed chuckle, cracked open his armpit. It was completely covered in bubblegum. I merely stared in amazement, then told an equally amazed auntie what her nephew had just done.

His reason: "I wanted to see if it would melt."

Vaguely remembering some recipe to get gum from a carpet, I told my sister to hang on a minute and proceeded to rub peanut butter all over Alex's sticky armpit, much to the amusement of all the children, who had gathered round to witness what big brother just did. The awe in their eyes made me warn them never to do this thoughtless thing themselves. Alex, looking thoughtful and absolutely guiltless, calmly stuck his finger in his armpit and started eating the peanut butter. Only his auntie and I were disgusted. The kids' estimation of their older brother grew yet another degree.

Chapter 18

HI SOCIETY

My sister and her husband invited us to a very fancy Opimian Society dinner held in the city one year. The Opimians are wine connoisseurs. We are not. Just the thought of sipping nice wine and eating out somewhere other than the local burger joint, where children can eat and then whoop and screech down whatever slides or tunnels thoughtful patrons might have provided, brought a ray of sunshine streaking in to our world.

I believe we said something like, "Yes. Thank you thank you, thank you. When?"

Seated at our oh-so-perfectly laid table on that oh-so-eagerly awaited evening the following week were my sister and her husband, and an elderly couple whom we had never met.

The theme was Spanish, the meal was catered exquisitely, and the wine was plentiful. While we sipped our Macabaeo Parellada D.O. Conca de Barbera 1994, I chatted to the gentleman seated on my right who, it turned out, owned a vineyard in Chile.

He was explaining the unique growing conditions in his

area that made his wine so very special when we were interrupted by a faint but persistent ringing in my purse. I had wrestled with the thought of turning my phone off so that I could enjoy a quiet evening, but settled instead with the threat to our eldest, who was the designated babysitter that night, that he was not to phone unless there was a death, or at least a lot of blood involved.

Excusing myself from the conversation, I leaned back and answered my phone. As I did so, I heard my sister politely explain, "It's one of her children. She has six, you know."

I listened as our son explained somewhat breathlessly that our dog, Molly, had just trotted up with one of our chickens in her mouth. Since both blood and death were involved, he figured he could call.

"Is it dead?" I asked. He replied that it most likely was. "Then pick it up by the feet and smack Molly over the head with it a few times," I said firmly, unaware of the sudden silence at the table beside me.

Alex protested that he couldn't touch the dead bird.

"Use rubber gloves then," I said with determination, explaining as an aside to my sister, "Seems Molly grabbed a chicken around the neck and killed it."

After arguing with Alex that Molly needed to be disciplined for her actions, our conversation was interrupted by his younger brother's breathless announcement, "The chicken just went buck-buck".

"Then put her back and lock the coop door," I said.

Alex said something that was lost to me by the sound of children yelling in the background.

"Tell the children to be quiet."

I pulled the phone from my ear as he delivered the directions in no uncertain terms to his siblings. When the noise diminished slightly, he repeated his question: Could he round the chickens up with the baseball bat?

Alex used the bat in the evening because he was nervous about the possibility of a coyote seeking a free chicken dinner.

"Use the bat if you have to, but don't hit any of them too hard," I sighed, unaware of the nervous glances beside me.

I signed off and calmly tucked into my paella, only to notice that no one else was eating. In the silence that ensued, I paused. Perhaps an explanation was in order here.

"It's Okay," I said to my sister. "Apparently Molly only stunned the bird. When Stanley tried to grab it with the gloves, it clucked and took off."

After a charged silence, the gentleman next to me said, "And Molly would be...?"

"Her middle child," my sister cut in smoothly, as my husband choked on his chorizo.

"My goodness," replied the elderly wife. "These new methods of child rearing never fail to amaze me. You must have" – she paused and gave a fleeting look at her husband, and then finished – "very unusual children."

I glanced at my sister, smiled thinly and said, "Oh, you should meet my sister's kids."

Thanks to karate lessons, the kids have now learned to count in Japanese. Yesterday while I was busy with the teller, the three youngest got bored sitting in the corner and next thing I knew Eddie was lying on the floor doing sit ups with Elly holding his feet and Stanley counting in Japanese: "Ichi, ni, san, chi, go…"

Chapter 19

THE SKUNK

A skunk struck last night. If ever there is a bad way of awakening, it is to have eau de skunk waft in your window at about 3 a.m. It clears your sinuses instantly and leaves you gasping under the covers. Fortunately it was not our dog that disturbed the little fellow – this time – she learned her lesson at approximately the same hour of the night, four months earlier that year. No, some silent night hunter took the chance on this occasion. Coincidentally, our power went off at about the same time. One wonders if some poor owl didn't fly, blind and gasping, into the power line. As Greg at that time relied upon an electric clock to awake, we woke late and the scramble began.

Two minutes in the shower was followed by a mad search for his brush. Remembering that there was an emergency brush in the van – there are after all, a lot of heads that usually need emergency brushing – I directed him there. He stepped out into the -20 degree winter darkness, opened the van door and leaped back in terror.

"There's a skunk in there!" he yelled.

"How can that be?" I replied from the porch. "It's been shut tight all night long."

"Well, it's around here somewhere," he insisted, nervously sniffing. Rejoining me, he said,

"You go get it. I can't afford to get sprayed."

I sensibly suggested he take the car that was parked beside the van instead. Peering anxiously, Greg made his way to the car, opened the door and yelled, "No! It's in here!"

The skunk must have danced, tail up and spinning that night, because both vehicles smelled for days.

After traveling in a stinky frozen car with frozen hair that was poking straight up, Greg arrived at work a half hour late, looking and smelling badly. He marched right past his surprised receptionist, through the waiting room and waiting patients without a sideways glance. It wasn't his best day.

For months he was very edgy around the yard, sniffing carefully before he approached the shed, woodpile or chicken coop – all favourite haunts of a skunk, according to our children's encyclopedia, which also said that skunks, contrary to popular belief, make good pets and eat vermin such as mice, lizards and snakes – all on Dad's current nasty list. The four-year-old twins, wildly excited at the prospect of a pet skunk, or "stunk" as they called it, raced wide-eyed for days to report a stunk sitting on the fence, a stunk under the deck and in the tree.

If there is a light spot to any of this drama, it came a few days later when, lying in bed one evening discussing the cons and pros and cons of a neighborhood skunk and why doesn't the darn thing hibernate anyway, my husband, after a contemplative silence said suddenly, "Isn't it a good thing skunks don't fly"?

1993:

March 30

Charles has a very bad cough, so while I was shopping, I picked up some children's cough drops. Charles of course bragged to the others about the "candy" he'd just finished.

"We want one too!" came a chorus of wails.

Frowning in Charles's direction I said, "Charles is sick. That's why he got one." Usually I'm smarter than that, but it was out before I thought.

Charles turned and said quietly out of the corner of his mouth, "Ya hafta cough first."

The hacking and coughing din that ensued was louder than a bingo hall at closing time.

June 24

We were driving in the van when suddenly Stanley asked, "Mom, is it today?"

Now here was a question I actually knew the answer to. "Yes," was my firm reply.

"Oh, thank doodness."

Thinking that I that this was the perfect opportunity to introduce my little son to the theory of time, I added "It is always today, Stanley."

"No," he replied with a shrug. "Sometimes it's tomorrow."

Chapter 20

WALK LIKE YOU KNOW WHERE YOU'RE GOING

The Fairmont Banff Springs has to be one of the loveliest hotels in the world. Built in the nineteen century, it is one of Canada's grand railway hotels, built in the Scottish Baronial style in our first national park, located in the Rockies.

One weekend the family decided to take the Springs up on a special they were offering and spend a couple of days in what we thought must surely be the very definition of luxury.

Well, it was luxurious. And very, very large. Scottish barons must have really liked a lot of corridors and ballrooms with big fireplaces because there were a lot of them there, and when you took a couple of turns, they all started looking the same. We managed to navigate the route to our spacious room because the chap at the desk kindly gave us a map. More than a few heads turned as we proceeded with six kids, all loaded down with backpacks and dragging their favourite blankets.

When we left the room, bound for the swimming pool, we accidentally left that map behind. I thought I knew where I was going, but after a few backtracks and turns, Greg took over and said somewhat peevishly, "Just follow me."

He marched off, and the rest of us had to move very quickly to keep up with his long strides. After jogging along in one direction for a time, I began to recognize a few landmarks, and it occurred to me that we might be heading in the wrong direction. However, he walked like he knew where he was going, so we gamely trotted after until, arriving at the final long ballroom and giant fireplace, we all came to a dead stop.

Puffing breathlessly with the kids, I looked at him accusingly.

"I figured you didn't know where you were going," I said testily.

"Well, then why did you follow me?"

"Because you walked like you knew where you were going" I said, arms folded.

And this, by the way, has been a catch phrase for us ever since. If you walk like you know where you're going, people will follow you. If you talk like you know what you're saying, people, particularly kids, will believe you. Well, that's a hopeful theory, and one that can be quite handy when employed to convince them of such things as their teeth falling out if they aren't brushed frequently, or hurting themselves if they leap off high objects. Kids just aren't afraid of things like that, which leads me back to our search for the pool.

When we finally found it – or rather them, as there was both an indoor and an outdoor pool at the hotel – we organised the kids so that each of the older ones had a younger one to watch, and each of us parents had all six to watch. As three of them could not yet swim, we were very careful to en-sure that they were with someone who could. And yet not careful enough, as once we were in the outdoor pool, Greg suddenly said,

"Where's Eddie?"

It gives one a very bad feeling to hear that.

We all gave a quick search, and then started calling. No response led to everyone in the pool suddenly looking around. Finally someone pointed up and said, "Is that him?"

And there was Eddie, perched on the lifeguard's chair, having climbed the tall ladder up. And he was getting ready to jump into about five feet of water below.

As I splashed toward the spot below the chair, Greg leaped out of the water and started to climb the ladder while both of us yelled, "Don't jump! Eddie, don't jump!"

Greg managed to coax the little waif back down the ladder, and when they got to the bottom, asked him, "Eddie, what were you thinking? You can't swim!"

With a shrug of his shoulders, he replied, "You woulda saved me, Dad."

There was just no fear. On his part anyway. Perhaps children frighten us because they have no fear.

I love that about them.

It sure takes a lot of faith to raise a parent through childhood.

Enter stage right: Eddie.

Stanley, crying off in the distance.

"If something happened to Stanley I wasn't there and it was an accident so I didn't do it."

Chapter 21

TONGUE FU

One year, our young son suffered an ear infection, which greatly reduced his hearing capacity. Coincidentally, I came down with laryngitis. Talk about your basic failure to communicate.

He asked, "What's for snacks?"

I said, "Popsicles."

"Hot pickles?" he replied, somewhat tentatively.

"Popsicles," I croaked, to a puzzled little face.

With this piece of misinformation, he marched off to inform a bewildered Dad just what Mom had concocted in the kitchen this time.

"What the heck are you feeding them now?" came the yell from the living room couch.

Popsicles have remained hot pickles to this very day.

When I asked our children, who were sitting in the bathtub gazing at the whirlpool formed as the water drained, just what they were looking at so intently, they informed me that they were looking at the "wormhole". Our gang called blueberries "blue bees" and caterpillars "killer pillers".

Merry-go-rounds became "mala-gala-goes" and bubble

gum the charming "gubble bum". The ever-popular spaghetti must have a dozen names in as many households. Ours is "bow-deddie". We still just call it "bow".

Ask any parent, and you will get the most marvelous assortment of unique words and phrases created by their children or grandchildren. A child's oral interpretation of an object or idea is often so fresh that it endures forever in the hearts and heads of their loved ones. These are living words – words packed with meaning and memory.

I love the memory of Charles lying on the carpet, watching particles of dust riding on a sunbeam, and suddenly saying, "Hey Mom, look – sun blasters!"

Sometimes the phrases children garble to one another are the best of all. Upon hearing that we were taking one of their younger sibling's urine to be analyzed, his older brother was overheard confidentially telling his buddy next door that his brother was going to have his pee hypnotized.

One year we took some Australian guests to visit the Banff area, including the beautiful Moraine Lake and the Valley of the Ten Peaks. Eddie, then five, rode in their car with their five-year-old daughter, Lauren. En route he announced to his contemporary that we were all going to the Valley of the Ten Pigs.

As we stood there gazing at the lovely scene, Lauren asked her mother, "Where are the ten pigs?"

Since Aussies pronounce "pigs" and "peaks" in a similar way, her mother just waved in the general direction and said, "Right over there, across the lake."

"How big are they, Mommy?" came the worried reply.

"Well, over three thousand meters, I should imagine," said her mother.

Lauren looked incredulously at Eddie-the-travel-guide, who seemed quite pleased with his first tour results.

It wasn't until she began having nightmares about giant Canadian pigs that the truth was sorted out.

For friends of ours, nail clippers will never be the same since they sent their wee daughter to fetch them. She came back with nipple clappers.

My sister's son whacked his elbow, started to howl, then stopped and gazed first at his arm, and then at his mother with a look of amazement.

"Now I know why they call it the 'ow bow!'" he said.

Perhaps in cases like this, rather than going to the dictionary to explain, one should get a blank page and start his or her own dictionary.

I've switched the cat's food to a brand called "Whiskas". Stanley told his teacher today that we were feeding the cat whiskey.

Upon hearing that a local store had been robbed, Charles quipped, "If I ever robbed a public store, I wouldn't take the money. I'd take the pickles."

Chapter 22

AUNTIE PAT'S PLACE

One of our favourite stopovers en route to and from summer camp each year is my sister Pat's place. Pat is an angel who welcomes us with open arms, gamely feeds us and gives the tribe a room to sleep in even though – for some unknown reason – just about every summer somebody gets sick. Last year when we wheeled in to Pat's and she ran out to meet us, I opened the van door and yelled, "Open the garbage, quick!"

She knew immediately what to expect and did so, just as Charles stumbled out of the van. And threw up on her foot.

This year we outdid ourselves as four of the kids came down with the flu bug. Pat was ready for us with a brave smile on her face. And boots. Once again I opened the window as we wheeled in and called out to open the garbage, however this time there was a significant improvement – bagged lunch. I had finally managed to catch the little *barfer* in time to pull over and give him the bag I now kept handy. He dutifully filled it.

That night I slept on the pull-out couch with my sister and we packed the six kids into her daughter's room. There was only one bed, so we tucked three into it, and put the others on the floor in their sleeping bags. At around 1 a.m. Charles wobbled downstairs and whispered the bad news: he'd been sick all over the bed. Not wanting to wake my sister, I groped my way quietly to the kitchen and fumbled through a cupboard for a bowl and spoon, and trudged up the stairs. To keep from waking the kids I managed in the dim room to move two of them from the bed, scrape the mess from the sheets into the bowl, and, step over many small bodies on the carpet to put the sheets in the wash. I then returned for the bowl and made my way to the bathroom toilet to tip the contents, turned on the light and discovered, to my horror, that in the kitchen I'd grabbed…a sieve.

1993:

April

Greg has been trying for some time now to teach Charles and Jane to blow their noses. The efforts have proven futile; they just don't want to part with the stuff.

After our usual stop at McDonald's this Sunday, Greg was driving while the kids were happily slurping on their ice cream cones. Jane, finishing first, bit off the end of her cone and sucked – noisily sucked – her ice cream out of the end of the cone. Greg, hearing the honk, brightened considerably and, dodging traffic, said, "Good blow, Jane! I knew you could do it!"

May 3

Greg finds driving in traffic stressful at best. When the kids are on board, the yelling from the back is often echoed from the driver's seat. It seems, however, that feelings are mutual.

I've been saying their prayers every night with the children, and Charles always says, "Save us from the time of travel."

I haven't the heart to correct him.

May 22

Traveling through town today we happened to pass a taxi driven by a Sikh wearing a turban. Eddie glanced once, then twice, then exclaimed, "Hey Mom! There's a GENIE driving that car!"

November

Elly, as she sped out the door, "I have my running shoes on AND my running coat!"

Chapter 23

CAMPING WITH THE CLAN

We have a nice farm. We have running water, electricity to work all those gadgets that make life easy, and cozy beds. We have a few acres with a dog to shoo away the coyotes, cats to eat the mice, and chickens that give us lovely eggs each day.

What else could one ask for?

The truth is, there isn't anything else. This is paradise. Now if you want to get philosophical about it, how do you know you're in paradise if you haven't experienced less-than-perfect conditions? This is the only reason I can think of that parents would willingly give up their solid roof and cozy beds to go camping with the kids.

Cramming eight people into a six-man tent with sleeping bags, sleeping mats, a significant amount of dusty clothing, shoes, coats, blankets, flashlights, and various toiletries is a very good way to discover how one might fall short of paradise; fall a long way in the other direction, in fact, which is what my husband's desperate whisper at 1 a.m. was alluding to as he swung at a mosquito and pushed yet another little foot out of his face.

"What the hell were we thinking?"

After attempting to prepare breakfast for the gang at the

campground I realized I hadn't really appreciated how nice a kitchen can be.

In the food box I'd assembled for the trip were those little packaged cereals the kids never get at home, and something called "Go-Gurt" that I purchased in a weak moment at the grocery store when one of the little guys insisted we should try something new and exciting for the camping trip. There was excitement – when it was discovered that I'd forgotten to bring milk and bowls and spoons. Luckily the little cereal boxes had perforations along the front so they could be opened and made into little cereal "bowls". Someone in the design department at Kellogg's was thinking of campers when they made these.

The Go-Gurt comes in a tube, so all you have to do is squirt it into the box, after you've squirted it at your sister, of course. The absence of spoons made eating these a bit of a challenge, but hey, what was another layer of stuff on your hands? It made it easier to hang onto the axe when you were chopping wood to light the fire to save the family from hypothermia.

The Kananaskis in the Alberta Rockies is a piece of paradise, and it was wonderful to wake up and gaze at the mountains through the mist of one's frozen breath. And throughout the day, one never failed to gasp in awe (not too big a gasp, or you could inhale enough mosquitoes to qualify as protein for the day) at their pristine beauty.

While my husband was taking the kids on an inspirational hike along forest trails, I hung back and tried to figure out how to prepare six boxes of Kraft Dinner in a pot that held about two liters of water. It took an hour to boil the water on a small canister of "Camp Gaz", by which time the gang was back. And hungry.

In order to speed up the process, I threw all six packs of the mixture in the water, and waited for it to come to the boil again. It didn't. I tossed in some butter, some of that very orange cheesy powder and stirred, which was not easy to do as a) there wasn't enough room in the pot to stir and b) the stuff was so stiff it wouldn't move.

One should never underestimate the power hunger has on the body. Those kids picked the macaroni out of that pot and ate it with only the briefest of negative remarks. It took a day or two for the orange stain to fade from their teeth and hands, and some of them complained of tummy aches, but at least they didn't demand seconds, which was a good thing, as there was no more Camp Gaz left.

My sister, who is a city dweller, is much older than I am. I do not mention this to irritate her, but to suggest that perhaps wisdom doth in fact accompany age. You see my sister and her husband happened to be camping at the same campground we were, only in a different section. They were "camping" with a group of friends who had trailers. Trailers are nice. They are little homes that you wheel out into the wilderness, and then wheel back when you are done enjoying the scenery. Moses should have tried trailers. We should have tried trailers.

Just after the macaroni affair, but before the prospect of a long afternoon of fun in the wilderness with the kids, my sister showed up at our camping spot and invited us over for "happy hour". The prospect of one happy hour in the day moved my husband and me to tears. The kids just said, "Oh, good! Food!"

Promptly at 3 o'clock, we showed up at the circle of trailers on the far side of the campground. Each trailer had a little awning, under which were some camp chairs and small tables that held magazines, books and refreshments. In the middle of the site were several picnic tables that had been drawn together, and upon which were seated my sister, her husband and friends – happy – just as they promised, enjoying snacks and liquid refreshments. There was paradise in the valley after all.

My husband and I sat down to cocktails and lovely little snacks that each camper had kindly contributed. The kids busied themselves with chips, pop and roasting marshmallows. I was enjoying the fine fare and friendly conversation so much that it was some time before I noticed our four-year-old twins, cheeks full, crawling around the picnic table.

"What are you chewing?" I casually asked

"Gum!" came the enthusiastic response. "There's a whole bunch under this table! Want some?"

Paradise, it seems, has its stickier side too. Perhaps paradise is just wherever you are, so long as you settle in with enthusiasm, and with vision unclouded by expectations. Trust, therefore, the child to find it.

Greg was late tonight so I found myself at the dinner table alone with the kids. We were proceeding nicely when suddenly Stanley began to howl and clutch his face. I looked over and was informed by his delighted siblings that his older brother had shoved a pea up his nose. My jerk reaction was to take a swing at Alex, who automatically used his arm to block me. He had, after all, been taking karate for several years. It stopped me dead in my tracks. What the heck was I doing, I asked myself, slapping my child? It was in that instant – I remember it as clearly as if it was yesterday – that I learned something that has served me for the rest of my life. I looked around at the kids and saw that they were struggling to keep a straight face and I realized that I had a choice here. I could blow up and make everyone miserable, or I could look at it for what it was - a funny situation that the kids would remember for a long while. A pea up the nose is quite funny for a kid. It didn't hurt Stanley's nose because he too was beginning to smile. What I learned in that instant was that I had a choice. I could yell, or I could give in and laugh. And laughter just feels so much better than anger. So I just started to laugh, and we all joined in, including Stanley when he finally managed to fish the pea out of his nose. It turned out to be a very happy supper hour.

When problems arise, I can't always change them, but I can change the way I react to them. I'll choose laughter any time I can.

1995

I guess it's time we had the sex talk. Or at least explained the – er – physiology of their pets.

Minnie the cat has already had two batches of kittens, which was a wonderful event in the house, but Greg and I figured that we'd just about exhausted all the friends and relatives we knew to give away more kittens, so we decided it was time to have her neutered.

Today, noticing that Molly the dog was in heat, I took her to be bred at a friend's place that had a German shepherd named Storm. I then pre-pared poor Minnie for the next day at the vet's: neither food nor drink for twelve hours.

This had Eddie totally confused, and though this would have been a very good time for that little talk, I didn't get that chance because his older, wiser brother, Charles, decided to do it himself.

Lifting his leg to ride an imaginary motorcycle, he twisted the imaginary handlebars and said, "It's easy, Eddie. Storm's gonna get his engine revved – pumped – you know. And Molly's gonna get her headlights turned on so that they just shine!" he finished with a drawl. "And Minnie, well" – he rolled his eyes sadly, then, crossing his arms he leaned forward dramatically –"hedge clippers!"

Chapter 24

VEGETARIANS

Driving in our old blue van one day with the three youngest children on board, I was jerked from my easy radio listening by our son Stanley who suddenly asked, "Mom, what am I?"

Now there are times when questions posed and answers given can make an indelible effect on the direction one pursues in life. I considered how to pose a simple response to such a deep philosophical question, and chased around such replies as "You are a child of God", or "You are Dad's and my love just all wrapped up together", but finally, tangled by my own metaphysical pondering, answered with firm authority, "You're a boy, Stanley."

"No, no," he replied. "I mean what kind of animal am I?" This reply had me even more confused and concerned than before. Had I missed something essential in their upbringing? Stanley continued, "You know, like a fish or something."

"Ah!"

Suddenly it was a little clearer what he meant, though I was a bit surprised that a seven-year-old considered these things. One could only imagine what he and his school buddies talked about. "Do you mean Zodiac? What sign were you born under?"

"Ya. So what am I?"

"Ya," chorused his brother Eddie from the seat next to him. "What are we?"

"Well, you are Aries," I said carefully, anticipating the next question before it arrived.

"What's an Aries?"

"An Aries is a ram."

A little silence ensued, and then Stanley said, "What's a ram?"

Before I could respond, Eddie perked up and answered, "I know! It's a sheep!"

I congratulated Eddie on his advanced vocabulary and left the two of them to figure out just what it might mean to be a sheep. Since I had no idea of what the ram represented, I thought it better just to say nothing and hope that my cryptic response met with silence. Luckily it did. For about a minute. Then the small voice of their voice of their five-year-old sister could be heard.

"So what am I?"

I was worried that she might ask this. "Well, you're a Virgo, Elly."

All three chirped, "What's a Virgo?"

"It's a virgin" I said, looking at them all levelly through the rear-view mirror.

"What's a virgin?"

Before I could even begin to wrestle with the pros and cons of having this conversation in a rolling vehicle in the middle of traffic, Eddie's arm shot up and he proudly said, "I know!"

I looked at him blankly, but had little time to either wonder or worry before he continued, "Can't eat meat!

Never regret anything that made you smile.

1995:

November

Frame this moment:

A tousled blondie walking through a morning sunbeam, ragged blanket over one shoulder, with a kitten scampering after her, batting at her pajamas and at the rags hanging off the blanket.

How does one capture the frame of this movie reel that is my life? I want to put it on pause and savor, savor, savor. So I pick up that little raggedy bundle, take her to a cozy spot, kiss her gently and tell her, "I love you", because love, you see, is eternal and a good verbal sprinkling whets the memory and freezes the frame forever in your heart.

Chapter 25

CHRISTMAS BIZARRE

Each year our church, like countless others, holds a Christmas bazaar to raise funds for their project of choice. This year Stanley and Eddie and their good buddy Evan were invited to be in charge of the fishpond. This does not involve real fish, but rather a heap of goodies and toys stashed behind a screen. When a prospective customer pays for the use of a fishing rod and casts it over the screen, it is the job of the chaps with the goodies to hook something to the end of the rod and give it two tugs. Presto, the fisherman then pulls up his rod and discovers what he got for fifty cents.

Our church is not a large one, and the bake table, dining room and fishpond all ended up in the same room. Since I happened to be on bake table duty at the same time the boys were on pond patrol, I was able to keep an eye on them as I sold baked goods.

The first hour progressed smoothly, with several customers lined up to try their luck with the fishing rod. It was in the second hour, when the crowd thinned out and the boys became restless, that trouble began.

Reverend Bob, noticing the lull, decided to try his hand at fishing, but unfortunately was not told all the rules of the game. When the lads tugged on the string he stood still and waited for something to happen. It did. A package of toys and candy flew through the air and hit him squarely between the eyes.

A short while later, something resembling a fish was procured, and the boys tried their hand at putting on an aquatic show, somewhat like a puppet show, with flying fish. This was followed by a flying duck that migrated in a westerly direction across to the dining room where it landed on a mince tart, causing some consternation on the part of the elderly lady eating it.

It was then suggested that the wee gents take a break.

I escorted them across the room to the dining table, where they joined their sisters who were practicing balancing spoons on the ends of their noses.

With the appearance of the lads, the balancing progressed to who could shove the end of the utensil the furthest distance up one's nostril; and from this to who could balance a spoon on the end of one's nose whilst drinking orange juice. The beverage in question produced an orange stained smile on their upper lip that, with the spoons on their noses, made them look for all the world like deranged koalas.

It was at this time that the flying duck mysteriously appeared on the table, launching the entire table into a chorus of "Rubber Ducky, You're The One".

A small scuffle over the last remaining hot dog was followed by a larger-scale battle over the beleaguered duck, which emerged from the scrum in a very squashed condition. When his younger sister started to howl, Eddie demonstrated his revival skills by blowing into a tiny hole in ducky's back end. Quite miraculously, the duck inflated. The response from the table over this feat encouraged him to repeat it, which kept him quiet for a time, since he managed to hyperventilate doing it.

It is difficult to discipline a table of children wearing spoons and wide orange smiles and singing "Deck the Halls", particularly when one is being watched by a roomful of grandmas.

A quiet suggestion was made that they go play outside. With a cheer and a scuffle for the door, they took the duck and played football with it for the remainder of my shift, the pond forgotten in the rush for a new game.

As I tucked them into bed that night, a thank-you was given to God for the great day at church. Eddie, eyes shut and with a smile in his voice added, "I'll bet You just can't wait till Evan and Stanley and me are the wise men in the Christmas pageant."

I'll just bet He can't.

Chapter 26

DOWNHILL DAY

We'd had better days on the mountain.

We lost one son's hat, his mittens, our daughter's hat, and our daughter.

Early on a Saturday in February, we loaded the old van with seven pairs of skis, boots and poles, five children and one of their buddies, and left for Sunshine Village in *Banff, Alberta*. We stopped briefly for gas on the highway, before heading westward. About five minutes later, our eldest son's buddy asked, "Where's your sister?", whereupon our son peered into the back seat, and asked the two lumps hidden under pillows and jackets, "Where's Elly?"

"Shhhh," was her brother's breathless reply, "we're hiding on her."

Summarily advised of the problem, I reacted with studied calm, and burned across the first piece of traversable ditch to the opposite side of the highway, proceeded in haste in an easterly direction, and took the first exit off the road, which took me at high speed in the wrong direction.

When we finally arrived at the service station, there was the little waif, arms crossed and fighting back tears. She threw open the van door and yelled, "You idiots!", which was a sentiment she shared at some length in the gondola going up to the ski hill for the benefit of any strangers who might be interested.

On the first run, the younger three took a short cut with their older brother, Charles, in order to meet me on our favourite hill. After waiting a half hour at the bottom for them, the latter showed up and explained that Stanley had accidentally slipped off the run, and since he was unable to get back up, they all jumped down to join him. Unfortunately, they failed to note in the process the little black diamond symbol beside that run.

I suggested that perhaps it would be a good idea to go back up there to see why they still weren't down, which, to his credit, Charles did.

Another half hour passed before all four arrived at the bottom, wearing a pound of snow on their toques. Seems that they had fallen in the middle of a very narrow traverse, and did a fair job of holding up traffic. Stanley, eyes wide, explained.

"I fell? And I couldn't get my ski back on? So Elly tried to help and lost hers too? So we just stayed there and this snowboard guy? He came around the corner and said the Oh-S word! Then his friends came? And they said it too!"

By this time I was so cold that I suggested we go into the lodge for a hot chocolate to warm up. The three younger ones came with me; their brother muttered something about needing to finally get some skiing in and went off in search of his older brother and friend.

Inside it was not much better. Just different.

The hot chocolate meant to warm them up did just that – from the outside. A full cup of it landed on two of them.

It takes a while to dry a snowsuit using only the hand dryer in the washroom, and by the time we were finished, it was lunchtime. After waiting another hour for the older three, who in the thrill of the downhill lost track of time, we ate our lunch.

Half the day was gone, and we had only skied one run when we exited the lodge, only to discover the loss of two toques and one pair of mittens.

We made do with parka hoods, but one cannot easily ski without mittens, so we scrounged a pair from a sympathetic attendant in the lost and found.

We chose a T-bar to get to the first run. Elly went solo, I followed and finally Stanley and his brother Eddie went up together. And came down separately. That is, Stanley fell off, knocking Eddie in the process. Eddie's coat got tangled on the bar, and he was dragged, shrieking with laughter, up the lift. The information eventually filtered down to the attendant, who stopped the lift, and both lads started over again.

When they resurfaced at the top, they decided that it would be a good idea to play a game of tag. The faint scent of cocoa trailed them as the two breezed by me, yelling, "Hi Mom! Elly's it!"

Elly followed, yelling, "I QUIT!"

"I quit too," the fellow I'd ridden up with said.

"Are those Bickersons yours?"

I smiled weakly and pointed myself downhill, which

pretty well summed up the day.

When we rejoined the others and crawled back into the van at the end of the afternoon, the younger three said, "Oh gee, Mom, that was just great! When can we come up again?"

I think I'll just wait until their Dad can take them. I really hate to have all the fun myself.

1995:

November

We were discussing our chickens today in the van. When I told them ours were only a year old, Stanley said, "I wonder what teenage chickens are like."

Upon hearing this, Charles perked up and, with one arm slowly snaking left, shoulders hunched, he flexed his shoulder blades open and shut and said, "Yo!..Buck!"

1996:

Elly just fell and hurt her knee. Though I carefully cleaned and bandaged it, the crying persisted. Finally I suggested that I could read a story – surely that would take away the sting.

"Just one?" she asked balefully. "That'll never work. It's a three story sting."

It is very windy today. The three youngest were outside when suddenly they came in, breathless with excitement, and said, "Do we have an umbrella?!"

1997:

September

Eddie, while peering into his bowl of Cheerios: "Mom, if Cheerios have holes in them, why don't they sink?"

Today at the dinner table, Stanley asked, "Mom, have you ever been a nun?"

Greg thought this was pretty funny. I was mystified. Turns out Stanley didn't really know what a nun was, but did know what they looked like because they looked after Problem Child II before he was released to the public.

Makes perfect sense now.

November

The kids have discovered a foolproof way to escape music practice: practice at home.

Our country school goes from K through 9. In grade 4, music is introduced. They start with the recorder, and progress through each grade till they get to junior high, at which time they get to pick which instrument they wish to torture their parents with. Of course it is wonderful to develop the brain fully, which apparently is what learning how to play music does.

Our kids weren't concerned about developing their brain – they were too smart to fall for that one – but they were clever enough to fear retribution from their music teacher who once a week was watching to see if they had something musical tucked under their arm when they got on the old yellow school bus. I too feared the music teacher. I remembered my music teacher from grade 7 and the trouble I got into with my alto horn. I never did take the time to learn to read music, so I used to fake it when the teacher struck up the band. I was encouraged to pursue another option in grade 8. So, with hope in my heart that today would be different from last week and that they could actually read the music, I would tell them it was time to practice.

And practice they did. At the same time. One can only listen so long to "Twinkle Twinkle Little Star" played by a recorder, two ukuleles, two trumpets, and a trombone before yelling, "Great, kids. That'll do for tonight!"

They've perfected the sober look, but I see that gleam of triumph in their eye as I sign their practice sheets every week.

Chapter 27

CHRISTMAS TREE

Christmas is truly a joyous time of the year. I have many, many happy memories of seasons past, however I am aware that I have what I call a selective memory. Because of this, I have taken to writing things down in a diary to remind me of what to avoid the next time around.

The following are notes from last year's Christmas tree episode.

December 1: Peruse neighborhood for a good cheap tree. Note grocery store where we bought last year's crooked yet bushy and beautiful tree has a new load of them. Check to see if this one is straighter than last year's disaster. Difficult to tell if it is straight when it is in a big net bag. Price is right, tree is, after all, bushy and beautiful. It's early, but we're keen. We buy it. Tree "stored" (tossed) in back yard where it is cool.

December 2–12: Unseasonably warm weather. Hope tree doesn't dry out.

December 13: Eldest son and I attempt to put up tree. Seem to recall some formula one added to the water to prolong the life of the tree involving sugar and bleach. To water we add quarter cup sugar and splash or two of bleach.

Tree eased into tree stand. It is not straight. Screws

tightened into tree do not hold it up. Son and I stuff tree stand with scraps of wood, rocks, pieces of a wooden puzzle that we find in the toy box, two pieces of bamboo. Tree still swaying. Two fishing hooks and some fishing line attach tree to air vent conveniently situated above tree. We have a nice carol fest with kids, vacuum up many needles, and decorate it.

December 14: Find tree on its side. Wet spot on carpet mopped up. Tree propped against wall. It doesn't look bad like that. What the heck. Attempt to find fishhooks. They seem to have flown up the vent. Add more water and a touch more sugar and bleach. Vacuum up a lot of needles. More carols sung.

December 17: Husband and son dissatisfied with leaning tree. After lengthy discussion, decide to duct tape lower branches to stand.

December 18: Tree once more in horizontal position. Wet spot mopped up. Many, many nails driven through stand, into tree trunk. More rocks and wood added. Broken bamboo and duct tape discarded. Carol or two hummed. Tree redecorated with remaining unbroken decorations.

December 19: Tree over again. Carpet soaked. More water added to reservoir. Tree propped against wall. Large quantities of needles vacuumed up. "Silent Night" tonight.

December 20: Husband bought new high-tech tree stand. Costs twice as much as tree. It works. Vacuum cleaner is broken. Carpet permanently stained. Perhaps a bit too much bleach? Tree redecorated, no carols sung.

December 26: Sing "Hark the Naked Conifer" and throw out tree along with a tree stand. It's Boxing Day. We're off to buy a synthetic tree.

Chapter 28

THE JEEP

City folk who move to the country often do so to live the dream, which usually includes something like the following: wide open spaces, fresh air, dogs, and tough trucks. When we moved to a small acreage many years ago, one of the things my husband, Greg, decided he really wanted was a tough truck. He found his dream in the advertising section of the *Calgary Herald*.

When he bought his 1977 Jeep Truck (from a fellow who immediately left town), it had no rear brakes, a hole in each gas tank (but then, only one was hooked up), a faulty manifold, a battery with two hours of life left in it, a gear shift that defied human effort, no gas gauge, no rear signal lights, and no speedometer. It had a new paint job applied lovingly with a brush over a lot of suspicious looking bumps. It was tough alright – tough for his wife to believe that he actually paid money for it.

There was, however, four-wheel drive, a roll bar and a winch, which was, he explained, what he really wanted for vicious winter weather. When it comes to weather, Greg's memory is long. His sensibility is correspondingly short, for he was worried that someone might steal that baby because, you see, one did not need a key to start it. One simply turned the keyhole and away it roared.

To be fair, it was worth something because it gave him and every one of his children so much driving pleasure.

Although he is a relatively calm Jekyll on country roads, my beloved redneck becomes a raging Mr. Hyde on city streets in our Chevy, tailgating as he fumes, "Drive that buggy or park it!" Not so when he is behind the wheel of the Jeep. The truck transforms him.

When he left the house for the inaugural cruise with our teenage son at his side, my husband, for whom Elton John can be a trifle strident, played rap music on high volume (in order to hear the radio above the noise of the engine, you have to have it cranked to the limit) with his window – the one that works – rolled down, and his shirt sleeves rolled up. The two of them wore a pair of smiles longer than the crack on the windshield.

They pulled into the Co-Op to fill up with gas. Noticing that the gas cap was locked, the attendant asked for the key, and was told, "Oops, sorry. Left them all at home." The baffled lad was told to "just yank on it", which seems to be the solution for most things on the truck, and which indeed produced the desired effect.

There is not one part of that old Jeep that has not been replaced or serviced. We took out the AMA's Deluxe Plus Gold Card, Tow-You-Anywhere, Fix-You-Anytime Service and have used it many, many times. I love the AMA.

I am on a first name basis with most of their tow truck drivers because the darn thing breaks down whenever I drive it. This is likely because when the Jeep sounds funny in the morning, Greg takes the Chevy to work.

I always get a bad feeling when I look out the window early in the day and see that truck parked there. On one occasion, I took it in and told our long-suffering mechanics that it was making a strange noise whenever I accelerated. When they looked under the hood and turned the ignition, the whole engine lifted up and almost out of the truck, putting the fan through the radiator. Almost lost my mechanics.

One day in a rainstorm, the windshield wiper took a few swipes and then just flew off. We still don't have one, but it's on the passenger side, so it doesn't matter so much.

The radio seems to work on its own mysterious schedule, suddenly blaring on maximum volume when we hit bumps, which happens frequently, as the shocks are gone. The kids love this, but it scares the wits out of the driver.

The exterior button on the door handle fell off too, and now we have to open the driver's door by going through the window.

The gas gauge doesn't work. Again. I've given up on it and just guess when it's empty. The other day I cruised in to the gas station and yelled, "fill 'er up!", only to have a puzzled attendant put in four dollars' worth of gas.

Then there was the summer when it wouldn't go in reverse or park, and started in drive. You had to be very careful that when you stopped, there was nobody in front of you and you were on a dead flat surface, as there was no emergency brake either.

Our mechanics did finally find a new gearshift, to accompany the new thermostat, fuel pump, carburetor, starter (second of three), various cables and belts, and lights.

In the summer when the heater blasts hot air, we put ice packs on our heads. In the winter when it blasts cold, we wear toques. When it snows, one has to get out and turn the hubs on the front tires to get it into four-wheel drive, which can be annoying at -35 degrees.

But it goes like stink. Speaking of which, there is usually some fine gravel in the back of it on cold days to throw on our hill when it gets slippery. Unfortunately, the cats discovered that gravel and, well, whenever there's a warm wind, the smell is nasty.

Our mechanics have christened it "the Road Warrior" and want to know why we still have it. I want to know too. My husband's reply is always, "Honey, we've fixed so many things on it that nothing more can go wrong." He's been saying that for two years now.

It smells, it roars, it jerks and bumps, and it takes a lot of unscheduled time off, but Greg and the kids will never let me forget that day of glory when the Suburban got stuck in a big drift on our hill, and the JEEP winched it out.

Oh, it is amazing alright. One of the most amazing things is that Greg's worst nightmare one day came true, and it was stolen from the parking lot. Considering that all the thief had to do was open the door and turn the key hole, the theft wasn't that difficult. What was amazing – for his wife – was that anyone would actually want to take it. My secret joy was short lived, however, when one of our mechanics spotted it at the other end of the city and called in to ask if we had sold it. It was forthwith retrieved, Greg was relieved, and it was then that I finally believed that we would never, ever be rid of it.

If anyone wants to buy a Jeep cheap, contact me.

Chapter 29

CHICKEN SOUP

I am very fond of chickens. Unfortunately, our pup, Ned, is very fond of chickens too, and made it his business last summer to eat all our laying hens.

It was a sad day when the last brown feather floated in the wind. My husband, ever the pragmatist, suggested that we take the opportunity of an empty hen house to buy meat birds and raise them to pack our freezer full of organic meat.

We did indeed seize the opportunity (carpe cluck), and in a matter of three short months, our chickens had reached a size that we deemed suitable for the pot. Not knowing how to go about the job of dispatching them, I sought the advice of neighbours who had done this before. Our friends Janet and Jordie told me that you set up a bar, get some tables, knives and, if possible, a chicken *plucker,* and you're in business.

Showing a firm grasp of the directions, I asked if you sat at the tables, paraded the birds across the bar, knifed them as they passed, then threw them in the *plucker.*

Well, it turns out the bar is for the people. You stock it with your favourite beverage, which you will need as you handle your assigned task. The tables are for the chickens, after they have met with the knife and been in the *plucker.*

Being raw rookies when it came to popping off poultry, we enlisted our faithful friends to help us, as well as Jack, the children's phys. ed. teacher, who we deemed suitably athletic for dispatch duty.

The delicate problem of how the children would react to the flock's demise was then addressed. One early childhood memory that is forever etched in my mind is a visit to our Uncle Tom's farm one Sunday. My uncle's family thought that city kids might get a kick out of seeing where Sunday dinner came from. I shall never forget the sight of a headless chicken pursuing my sister around the farmyard, made all the more nightmarish by the fact that no matter which way she turned, the darn thing followed her.

We warned the children that the spectacle of a chicken flipping around without a head might prove to be a worrisome sight, or worse, could permanently put them off chicken dinners. Their reaction was to invite the neighbour children over, and then fight for the best seats for their version of *A View to a Kill."* Choosing the pitched roof of the coop, they perched on top, breathless with anticipation.

It took Jack, who drew axe duty, a few whacks to finally sever the first chicken's head. The body was then tossed into the long grass, where it gave a few flips and twitches, and lay still.

Six pairs of wide eyes slowly filled with disappointment. After a brief silence, our son Stanley spoke for them all. "That's it?"

Jack, noting the children's dismay, suggested they wait for the next one. The sight of their teacher chasing forty panicked poultry around the coop brought more squeals than the ensuing termination, as number two flopped and dropped. The third chicken somehow managed to cluck without its head, which proved to be the highlight of the show.

With not enough blood and gore to engage them, the children soon tired of their perches, and returned to their games. All, that is, except for our nine-year-old son, Eddie, who convinced his teacher to let him have a go at rounding up the chickens.

He caught them dashing into corners, cowering on perches and in mid-flight. There was not a bird that could escape the lad.

For our convenience, Jordie brought his *plucker*, which is a useful tool that looks like a washing machine that has its inside lined with rubber nipples. One merely dunked the bird in a large tub of boiling water to loosen the feathers, then hung it over the rotating nipples until most of the feathers fell off, remaining mindful at all times that one's own nethermost parts did not brush the contraption.

From there it was to the gutting table, where the women – who had drawn the short straw – got the task of removing innards. This we did on newspaper, the intent being that after each bird was done, you rolled up the offal paper and pitched it in the rubbish bin. The system worked well but for one small flaw: the newsprint came off on the bird.

One bird sported the headline "Off Ut Run" while another advertised athletic bras. Seems our organic chickens were wearing a layer of lead ink.

"Don't worry, it won't hurt ya," was Jordie's response. "It'll give ya something to think about while you're chewing."

It turns out that the best advice of the day was to set up the bar. Frozen margaritas helped turn what might have been a gruesome task into a marginally tolerable one.

After wrestling with a particularly stubborn gizzard, a frosty sip and a mumbled "Arri-ba!" helped ease tension.

By the end of the afternoon, we were all pretty well eased, and the birds were all pretty well stiff. Their white carcasses floated in a garbage can full of icy water.

As I leaned over to read the headline "oin th Club", the designated chicken catcher breezed in and announced, with a puffed chest and glowing eyes, "Mom, when I grow up, I'm going to be a professional chicken catcher!"

If that's the case, he'll have to find new co-workers. The thrill of the pluck is gone.

1999:

Charles shaved his first mustache today – or rather, had it shaved. Greg's been eyeing that little dark shadow for months and finally cracked, dragging his young son to the bathroom.

"He just went nuts Mom, that's all I can say," said Charles, followed by Daddy, who looked very pleased with himself. "He just squirted shaving cream all over my lip and got me with the razor!"

Chapter 30

HOLLYWOOD

For those who watched Jackie Chan in his martial arts film entitled *Shanghai Noon*, it might be of interest to note that the majority of the movie was filmed around Alberta in the area surrounding Calgary, Canmore and Drumheller.

Our ten-year-old son Eddie had the vast good fortune of being cast as a farm boy in the film; notoriety that, alas, never came to fruition on the silver screen, as his small episode ended up on the cutting room floor. However, the bug hit our family big time, and soon all our kids were demanding an agent. Shortly thereafter, Eddie had yet another audition. This time it was for a movie that was to take place in small-town Nebraska (once again to be filmed in Alberta) and in which a children's talent show was to be featured.

Now Eddie has a rather unusual talent. He can jump very high, do the splits in midair and land, then repeat this in rapid succession. His new agent thought that this talent was just bizarre enough to win him some recognition. However, when he got the call to go, his father, ever vigilant to maintain fairness and equal opportunity in the family, demanded that his brother Stanley get his day in the spotlight too.

Now Stanley is not the acrobat that his brother is. His specialty at the time was blowing into his hand to make rude raspberry noises. And so it was deemed that Stanley would be Eddie' accompanist.

We are still not sure how we got the agent to agree to this. My only thought was that she was very busy that day, and when I explained their routine on the phone, she wasn't really paying much attention. She just said, "I'm sure they will both do just fine", and gave me the address of the downtown hotel that was hosting the auditions.

During the drive into the city that evening, Stanley expressed some doubt as to just how their routine would be received. Eddie, now the seasoned actor, coached his brother. "Just relax. They like you lookin' natural." Just how natural a farting jumping bean might appear was something I myself was pondering.

We arrived a bit early and stood outside the hotel room where auditions were taking place. From inside we could hear a piano accompanying a child singing a lovely folk song. Stanley shot a short, nervous glance at his brother and said, "Uh-oh."

Once inside, the boys were told to line up in front of a desk where two no-nonsense women were sitting with sheets of paper in front of them. In the corner of the room was a chap leaning behind a large film camera.

"Just say your names and what it is you are going to do," one of the women said crisply.

Eddie, standing stiff with eyes wide as two golf balls said very quickly, "I'm Eddie and I'm gonna do my jumping thing."

"And I'm Stanley and I'm… uh… I'm…." Stanley looked wildly at me for a clue.

"The accompanist," I whispered, grasping for a word.

"I'm the accompanist," he said.

I smiled encouragingly and gave them the thumbs-up sign.

And so began one minute of extraordinary talent. As the camera rolled, Eddie leaped and Stanley blew loudly into his hand. They stopped when Eddie ran out of air, and both stood with shoulders heaving as they fought to catch their breaths.

Stunned silence filled the room. Finally Stanley shrugged his shoulders and said, "That's it."

"Well", said one woman, somewhat unsteadily. "That's certainly… er… novel."

It turned out that their greatest fan was the cameraman, who, wiping tears from his eyes choked, "That's the best thing I've seen all night!"

After being told, "Don't call us, we'll call you", which coincidentally was what our agent later said, we left and laughed all the way back to the farm.

Apparently Nebraska kids don't do that sort of thing for talent shows. Maybe they should come to Alberta some time.

February

Today, before I had time to blow out the candles on my cake, Eddie appeared with a marshmallow on a fork, and began roasting it over the bon-fire.

Chapter 31

DISNEYLAND

This was the year it came true for the kids – their dream of Disneyland finally arrived. The dream was not without a touch of sadness, however, as Greg announced that he could not come. Just a week off work would have put us in the red, and debt was not an option.

When we dropped Greg off at work en route to the airport, Stanley was in tears. His dad took him by the shoulders, pointed him at a mirror and said, "Stanley, each day you need to look in the mirror and say these words:

'This is the day that the Lord hath made. We will rejoice and be glad in it.'"

Greg made him repeat it and – magically – the tears dried up.

There were many moments to remember.

On the plane:

The kids wondering how many times they could press what they called "the room service button" above their heads.

Stanley saying "Yes!" to everything that passed by on the

plane and ending up with the *Financial Times,* which he dutifully attempted to read. Eddie, upon the approach to the airport yelling "Mom, there are PALM TREES OUT THERE!"

The view of the Hollywood sign on the hill as we touched down, and six pairs of eyes widening in wonder and joy.

On the road:

Just as we entered the chaos of an L.A. freeway in our rented seven-seater van, Alex turning on the radio to hear it suddenly blast forth with the Beach Boys belting out "California Girls".

Alex's calm navigation on the freeways that always got us where we needed to be. At fourteen he quite literally knew where he was headed.

Palm Desert:

Stanley trying to sneak up on the flamingos to fluff their feathers.

Endless rounds of grounders in the playground. Funions with their friend Nick.

At Disneyland:

Pulling up to the Toon Town station on the train first thing in the morning, watching a choir warm up and all of a sudden hearing a woman belt out in a glorious voice, "This is the day that the Lord has made! We will rejoice and be glad in it!" and then slowly pulling out of the station, as the rest of the choir joined their voices to stir our hearts.

This morning our young teen, Charles grabbed the hair gel, which was beside the acne-fighting Aloe Vera gel, and smeared it on his face.

Muttering, he rinsed it off, cruised into the kitchen and grabbed a bagel. After eating most of it, he marched off and tossed the crust down the laundry chute. After staring for a moment at both the chute and his perplexed mother, he shrugged and said, "Ah! I'm losing my mind!"

Chapter 32

FAMILY DAY

One of the positive lasting gifts that Premier Ralph Klein gave Alberta, before he left office, was an extra day of vacation. Since there are no holidays in February, our government decided to invent one. They called it Family Day.

In the spirit of the day, our family contemplated various family vocations that might please everyone. The boys vetoed shopping, but managed to convince us to play football that first year. They outnumber the girls five to three. We didn't stand a chance.

To actually get something resembling a team together, we called up my husband's brother, his family and friends, and convinced them that since the weather was so unseasonably warm, they should have a game with us.

We were the only ones on the high school football field on that bright sunny Monday afternoon, playing touch football with three oldies, six teens, and three little guys. Somehow the teens ended up together on one team, forcing the rest of us to teach them a lesson.

There were lessons:

Number 1: Although a prairie football field in winter may look bare and inviting, the ground is frozen solid under it, and there is a lot of hidden ice underfoot.

Number 2: Small folks are fast, and old folks used to be and still think they are and so try to be.

Number 3: The human body has many, many muscles, and many, many are not often used.

We lost, but only just. The score was 86 to 35.

By the time we drove back to the house, my body was completely seized and I had considerable trouble getting onto a couch in front of the television. Showing sympathy for my complaints, my husband quipped, "Hey honey, there can't be many old broads out there playing football. You should feel proud of yourself."

I was feeling sorry for myself as a matter of fact. And increasingly stiffer.

My sister-in-law cheered us all up by procuring a bag of carrots and a large stash of junk food (you choose) and turning on Oprah Winfrey.

Oprah did a lot to cheer many of us up, because she was broadcasting from Nassau in the Bahamas at a beautiful resort. Her program? A contest to select the "Sexiest Man in the Caribbean." (Gasp.)

When Greg limped through and asked if we were ready to leave yet, our daughter threw her hands back against the couch and said, with more conviction than you would credit a thirteen-year-old with having, "We're not moving!"

And so we sat and watched as eight very scantily clad men paraded by and flexed all those muscles I didn't know we had. The women in the audience – and in our room – were very appreciative. My brother-in-law however, took it upon himself to explain a few things.

"The upkeep on those bodies is incredible." His voice was muffled somewhat by the fistful of chips he had just popped into his mouth.

"I mean, do you know how much work it takes to get that way?"

"Ya," I heard my daughter say absently.

"Why, they probably don't do anything else!" he added.

"Oh, I'm sure they keep busy with a lot of thing," was his wife's dry reply.

When the King of the Caribbean was finally crowned, and the last chip and cheesie downed, it was time to leave.

"I like Family Day," said one of our youngest. "Every day should be Family Day."

"It is," I grunted, as the crane was lowered to pull me out of the couch. "But sometimes on Family Day, Moms and Dads act like kids and then it takes them a long, long time to recover – their body and their memory. That's why we only really celebrate it once a year."

Chapter 33

THE COSTUME

Halloween is a child's favourite time. What's not to like? You get to dress up, and people give you candy that you can stash under your bed and eat for weeks.

It may be bad for your health, your teeth, your brain and your pocketbook, but Halloween is something we continue to celebrate just because it is fun. Besides, who can resist those wee bunnies and ballerinas who come to your door each year? It's those giant rabbits and suspect pirates who loom over the door and assure you that they are only in grade 7 that make one a tad nervous at times. I have a couple of them in my house.

My twelfth grader had a disguise for school this year, as did his college-aged brother. He wore a costume that I made for the kids twenty years ago, and that, unbelievably, still fits. You make the sheet big enough and it will fit over anyone's head. His brother taped a dill pickle to his upper lip and went as "crazy pickle mustache man".

When our children were young, the hot topic in the house was what they were going to be that year. When we were kids, we just made our own costumes. Doggedly following tradition, I decided that our household members would also make their own costumes. The older ones stuck to drag queens and rock stars, which apparently they could assemble themselves upon a visit to their parents' closet.

The little ones sometimes asked mom to help, which I did. The results usually looked fairly suspect, but the kids didn't seem to mind. Each year I made something – er – different.

We used a very large box, some yellow paint, and a poster of Sponge Bob Square Pants to recreate that cartoon character one year. Then there was the old *Slimer* outfit that our college lad just wore. It consisted of some slippery green material, two holes cut for eyes, and a wad of pink material resembling a tongue glued and sewed on for good measure. It has been in the dress up box for years.

One year we had the two-headed monster, suitable for twins. That one was made with some furry purple material I found on sale, and I then simply cut two holes in it for heads to poke through – they got to wear makeup to make them look fierce. Kids really like makeup, particularly if they can get their hands on it and decorate the bathroom too.

Sometimes I could recycle the costumes, if they held up between seasons. A bat became a mouse the following year when we took off the wings. The turtle suit I made became a grasshopper the next year, after we took the shell off. No one was really certain what our son was supposed to be, mind you, but it looked weird enough to be out on the street with at night, so we used it.

There was one outfit that didn't make the grade for recycling, however, and that was my most ambitious, and disastrous, costume of all. I actually bought a book that showed me how to make it. It was supposed to be an elf with legs dangling over a toadstool. What it ended up looking like was a pregnant pink and white cow with very large udders. Jane, bless her heart, wore it to school. The reaction from teachers was cautious puzzlement. Her friends were just amazed. By the end of the day Jane was just tired – of explaining what it was she was supposed to be, and of standing all day because with the large stuffed pillow thing that was supposed to be the mushroom around her waist, couldn't fit behind her desk.

Nowadays, a person can just go to the store and buy a cute little costume for a decent price. If you think ahead – way ahead – you can buy next year's costume at half the price, a week after Halloween is over. That's when the candy is on sale too. Makes good stocking stuffers. If you can keep it hidden that long.

Chapter 34

SPRING HILL

Spring on the prairies is a changeable feast. Sometimes it is so subtle that you barely notice winter is gone until one day you wake up and there's a dandelion on the south side of the house. Other times it screeches in at eighty kilometers per hour, slams to a halt and BOOM! Next day, there it is.

That is what happened this year. Serenaded by euphoric chickadees, we found ourselves dealing with Lake Erie on the lower five and Niagara on the hill.

A word about the hill. In order to get up to our house, one must navigate a very long, very steep hill that has a north face. Nice in the summer when the trees shade it, but a demon in the winter. Each year, many, many folks get stuck on the hill – mostly trying to back down when they have spun out on the ice that always builds up from folks spinning their tires. Usually they end up in the ditch in deep snow, but occasionally they tear through the hedge we planted to hide the very steep downward slope, and then teeter over the abyss. We've had two actually descend into the abyss, and it took two cranes all day to get them out. God Bless the AMA who never give up.

We've never actually had anyone die on the hill, however the debate is still out over the demise of the old pizza man.

He was the only guy who would attempt to deliver anything to our house. Then one day when we called up, someone at the shop – after we gave them our name and location – said 'so sorry, the guy died. No more deliveries for you.' As I said, it's a tough hill. We, on the other hand, almost never have a problem getting up because we have learned that the only way up is with four-wheel drive. Snow tires help considerably.

On this particular slam-bam spring day, due to the fast melt there was a river running down the road over thick ice. The old Suburban got half way up and started floating backward at high speed. This was not a good feeling as there is a killer bend in the road at the bottom. That current just swept us around it and we ended up beside the road in a wet, sticky snowdrift. Unfortunately, not only Jane and Charles, but also Grannie were along for the ride today. Grannie never even blinked when I helped her out of the car and told her we would have to walk. I don't think her unblinking eyes were paralyzed with fear -– no, Grannie is made of sterner stuff. At ninety-five years of age, she stepped right out and we began the slippery slope to home. The kids, who were wearing shoes, took turns going up, shrieking and slipping back down, but grannie and I – sensibly booted - just held on to one another and slowly, slowly marched upward. When we finally got to the top, Jane and Charles were shaking with both laughter and, being soaked, what was likely the initial stages of hypothermia.

Grannie just chuckled and said, "Well, THAT was certainly a challenge!"

They don't make them like that anymore.

.

Alex just cruised in looking for breakfast. He poured himself a bowl of cereal only to be informed the only milk we have is something called Rice Dream. The cereal was summarily dumped back in the box.

"We got any bread for toast?" he countered crankily.

"Er, no," I muttered as I popped a piece of cranberry fudge I'd been snacking on into my mouth.

"Okay. Let's see now. No milk, no toast. Just what do you suggest?"

"Fudge" I mouthed through sticky teeth, licking my fingers carefully.

"Fudge," he repeated, with flat disbelief. "You're giving me fudge for breakfast. Mom. I'm a growing teenager. I need meat. I need carbohydrates."

"There are cranberries in the fudge," I retorted calmly. "I know they're good for you."

"Whatever happened to the tofu and beets?" he said, now righteously scrambling a couple of eggs.

"This is your new evil mom," I said with a sticky smile.

In a couple of minutes, my protein-starved teen joined me at the table with his scrambled eggs. And a large piece of cranberry fudge.

What can I say – after all these years…busted.

Chapter 35

NO BROW, BRO

The body is a wondrous creation. We know that it is composed of countless vital interdependent parts, however there are a few parts that can get one wondering just what God had in mind when He added them on. Take, for instance, the appendix. What was He thinking when He tacked that little dangly thing onto a corner of the intestine? A person can easily live without it, but do something to annoy it – and no one knows exactly what it is that annoys an appendix – and you could certainly die from it. We almost lost a daughter that way. She was saved by the expert hands of a surgeon. We are eternally grateful.

One day while visiting friends, Eddie and Stanley found themselves contemplating the value of yet another body part. What, they wondered, were eyebrows for? You could wiggle them, raise and lower them, and some folks could even raise one and lower the other at the same time. Some men had wild, bushy brows, and, for reasons far beyond the understanding of lads of seventeen, some women actually plucked their eyebrows. Sure, they are interesting additions to the face, but it is doubtful that a person would die from an inflamed eyebrow.

The musings continued, and one thing led to the next and

before you knew it, the razor blade came out. What, they wondered, would a person look like without eyebrows?

When they arrived home, I greeted the lads with a hug, took a step or two away, and paused. They were grinning.

"What?" I demanded.

"Notice anything different, Mom?"

I confess that it took me a moment or two before I figured out what was different about Eddie. He looked like an alien who didn't quite get his earth disguise right. His ears and nose were there, but where were the brows?

What began as a simple lark one lazy afternoon had long-lasting effects. Those brows took quite some time to grow back in, during which time he gained notoriety at high school as "the kid with no brows".

One thing that Eddie had not anticipated was the fact that his look was always deadpan. Try looking surprised or angry with no eyebrows. Always there to help in a time of trouble, his siblings gathered and soon fixed the problem – with a felt pen.

"How are you feeling today, Eddie?" they would ask, and then would get to work. Some days he had the surprised brows that shot up into his hair like two exclamation marks. Other times the black lines came down to meet menacingly at the bridge of his nose. Horizontal lines were the determined look meant for math exams. If he couldn't make up his mind, he might end up with "the combo" – one arched and one normal brow – that made him look like he was thinking "Oh, really?" all day long.

As amusing as it was to keep the artists in the family busy, Eddie denied their advances with the razor when the eyebrows finally did reappear. It took about a week until there was any sign of a whisker over the eye. It was almost a month before one could identify a pattern that resembled an eyebrow.

Sometime later I caught my husband Greg exiting the bathroom with an amused grin on his face. "What now?" I asked.

"He's in there with the razor" Greg said. In answer to my worried look, he added, "Don't worry. This time he's searching for a legitimate whisker to attack with it. He claims he found one on his chin. Better get the Band-Aids ready."

2003:

Jane is getting desperate. She is about to graduate from high school and still has no idea what her future career might be. She took a test at school to determine possible careers, and the computer came back with plumber, framer, taxidermist.

And now the challenge begins.

The following pages are all yours. Write down those funny things your children say and do, for if you don't, you'll forget and regret.

Do it so that you may one day share the laughter and the love, and show your children just how important they have always been in your life.

"It may be that when we no longer know which way to go that we have come to our real journey. The mind that is not baffled is not employed. The impeded stream is the one that sings."

-Wendell Berry

Notes

Notes

Notes